SIMPLY
MANAGEMENT

SIMPLY MANAGEMENT

A CEO's Approach to Daily Effectiveness and Lasting Success

Martin Richenhagen

iUniverse LLC
Bloomington

Simply Management
A CEO's Approach to Daily Effectiveness and Lasting Success

The examples and scenarios that appear throughout this book are intended for purposes of illustrating true-to-life business situations; they are not expressions of actual events. All names, incidents, places, organizations (other than AGCO), and dialogue used in these examples were created for the instructional purposes of this book.

The information, ideas, and suggestions in this book are not intended to render professional advice. Neither the author nor the publisher shall be liable or responsible for any loss or damage allegedly arising as a consequence of your use or application of any information or suggestions in this book.

iUniverse books may be ordered through booksellers or by contacting:

iUniverse LLC
1663 Liberty Drive
Bloomington, IN 47403
www.iuniverse.com
1-800-Authors (1-800-288-4677)

Because of the dynamic nature of the Internet, any web addresses or links contained in this book may have changed since publication and may no longer be valid. The views expressed in this work are solely those of the author and do not necessarily reflect the views of the publisher, and the publisher hereby disclaims any responsibility for them.

Any people depicted in stock imagery provided by Thinkstock are models, and such images are being used for illustrative purposes only.
Certain stock imagery © Thinkstock.

ISBN: 978-1-4759-9476-6 (sc)
ISBN: 978-1-4759-9477-3 (hc)
ISBN: 978-1-4759-9478-0 (ebk)

Library of Congress Control Number: 2013910829

Printed in the United States of America

iUniverse rev. date: 08/12/2013

For my children Mechthild, Martin, and Stefan

CONTENTS

List of Tables/Illustrations xi

Foreword xiii

Preface xv

Introduction xvii

1. **The Essence of Management** 1

Definition of Management 1
True-to-Life Business Scenario: Focusing on
Managerial Tasks by Delegating Expert Responsibilities 2
Management Control Loop 3
Expert versus Management Tasks 4
Balance of Time Distribution between
Management Tasks and Expert Tasks 5
Management Styles 9
Situational Management 10
Basic Styles of Management Behavior 13
Management Styles in Daily Situations 13
Applying What You Have Learned 14

2. **Strategic Planning and Goal Setting** 15

Definition of Strategic Planning and Goal Setting 15
True-to-Life Business Scenario: Strategic Planning
and Goal Setting as a Group Process 16
Strategic Planning Tools 18
Establishing a Goal-Setting and Strategic-Planning Process ... 19

Planning Techniques: How Do We Get There from Here? 24
The Manager's Role 25
    The Most Common Obstacles to Goal Setting
    and Strategic Planning 26
Goal Alignment 27
    Collaborative Planning 27
    Planning Responsibilities 29
Change Management Definition 29
The Change Management Plan 30
Applying What You Have Learned 31

3.   **Organizational Structure** **33**

Definition of Organizational Structure 33
True-to-Life Business Scenario: Global Matrix
Organizational Structure 34
Types of Organizations 37
    Triangle Principle 37
    Decentralization versus Centralization 38
    Organizational Day-to-Day Operations 40
Virtual Team 51
    Effective Organizational Structure in the
    World of Working Remotely 52
Applying What You Have Learned 53

4.   **Governance and Controls** **54**

Definition of Governance and Controls 54
True-to-Life Business Scenario: Effective
Governance and Controls Are Key to Company Success 55
Purpose and Importance of Governance and Controls 56
Governance Methods and Measurements 57
    Governance Framework 57
    Principles of Governance 59
    Governance Results 62
    Requirements of an Effective Governance System 63
Controls Methods and Measurements 64
    Principles of Controls 64

Requirements of an Effective Controls System 66
Applying What You Have Learned...67

5.   **Employee Development and Advancement** **68**

Definition of Employee Development and Advancement..............68
True-to-Life Business Scenario: Effective and
Ineffective Methods of Employee Development 69
    Effective Method of Employee Development...........................69
    Ineffective Method of Employee Development........................70
Employee-Development Methods and Measurements 71
    Essential Development Methods...72
    Essential Development Measurements......................................74
    Basics of Employee Advancement..82
Employee-Development Obstacles 83
    Lack of Consistency between Set Goals and
    Development/Advancement...84
    Overuse of Central Training Departments...............................84
    Overemphasis of Expert Skills;
    Underemphasis of Challenging Opportunities 84
Handling Difficult Conversations: Some Tips for
More-Productive Development and Advancement Talks............85
Applying What You Have Learned...87

6.   **Communication**..**89**

Definition of Communication..89
True-to-Life Business Scenario: Effective Methods
of Strategic Communication 90
Twenty-First-Century Communication 93
    Technology and Effective Communication 94
    Virtual Teams and Effective Communication 97
Choosing the Right Method of Communication 98
Communication Guidelines.. 100
    Principles of Communication 100
Communication Plans 102
    Communication as a Management Tool 102
Applying What You Have Learned.. 103

7. **Motivation**..**105**

    Definition of Motivation 105
    True-to-Life Business Scenario: Effective Methods
    of Motivating Employees.. 106
    Motivation Models 109
        Abraham Maslow's Model.. 109
        Frederick Herzberg's Model..................................... 114
        Practical Application of the Herzberg Model....................... 115
        Daniel Pink's *Drive* Model 116
    Applying What You Have Learned................................... 119

Conclusion 121
References... 127
About the Author 129
About AGCO 131
Index 133

LIST OF TABLES/ILLUSTRATIONS

Figure 1-1: Management Control Loop...3
Figure 1-2: Balance between Management Tasks and Expert Tasks...........4
Figure 1-3: Less-Effective Time Distribution between Management
            and Expert Tasks 6
Figure 1-4: Too Much Focus Placed on Expert Tasks.........................8
Figure 1-5: Task and Relationship Orientation 12
Strategic Planning Tools 18
Goal-Setting and Strategic-Planning Process Model.......................20
Figure 3-1: Less-Effective Old Structure (Silos)...........................35
Figure 3-2: More-Effective Matrix Structure 36
Figure 3-3: Management Triangle..37
Figure 3-4: Functional Organizational Structure 43
Figure 4-1: Governance Process...58
Figure 4-2: Management by Exception..60
Examples of Breaches of the Governance System 61
Example of Areas Where Management by Exception Is Effective 61
Principles of Controls 64
Figure 4-3: Controls Process..65
Measurement Criteria...75
Evaluation Process..78
General Perceptions 79
Dealing with Conflict/Ambiguity 79
Problem Solving...80
Providing Advice 81
Respect for Others..81
Strategic Communication Plan..92
E-mail Essentials..96

Communication Goals 99
Key Components of Effective/Strategic Communication Plans 102
Figure 7-1: Maslow's Hierarchy of Needs.. 110
Self-Actualization Needs 111
Self-Esteem Needs.. 112
Belongingness Needs 112
Security Needs 113
Physiological Needs 113
Motivator-Hygiene Theory... 114
Core Statements: Management Wisdom for Every Day........................... 122

FOREWORD

As president and CEO of the US Chamber of Commerce, my focus has been to aggressively advance the competitiveness of US business. Expanding exports, strengthening capital markets, forging a national energy strategy, reforming health care and education, and protecting intellectual property rights are all critical aspects of a robust business environment.

However, none of these areas can truly be advanced globally or in organizations without a strong management foundation. Management has various aspects and components—finance, strategy, and planning, to name a few—but the most important of all is people. Hundreds of textbooks have been written on the subject of management in an attempt to reduce it to a science or a born skill. Yet despite all those efforts, successful management can be simplified into a few key factors. By design, management is a process that achieves a desired outcome through clarity in goal setting, feedback, employee development, and team motivation.

The rise of management as an organizational discipline was one of the most important business developments of the twentieth century. Management practices came into demand when labor transitioned from manual work to "knowledge" work. In the early 1900s, 90 percent of those employed anywhere in the world worked at blue-collar or domestic-service jobs. As economies and businesses grew, however, the need for skilled professionals grew as well. "Knowledge workers" carry their capabilities with them; they "own their means of production." And as companies sought to compete on a basis other than cost, the quality and efficiency of their managers became the "competitive advantage" that could set one firm apart from the others. In the twenty-first century, management efficiency will be even more essential, as knowledge and data become increasingly valuable.

Management is essential in all complex organizations that rely on people to make indispensable contributions. Managers direct workers to ensure that all their actions directly support the organization's purposes. Throughout *Simply Management*, Martin Richenhagen shares his experience and wisdom regarding the basics of strong management, particularly the ways in which combining all the tools of leadership work together to create a successful organization. From setting goals, to establishing governance and controls, to encouraging employee development and advancement, to using communication, delegating, and motivation, *Simply Management* offers effective techniques that will help organizations truly get to the next level.

The universally applicable approach outlined in *Simply Management* makes this book a key addition to any library for newly appointed managers and seasoned leaders alike. It is worth several readings to leverage the best of what Martin Richenhagen has to offer.

—Thomas J. Donohue
President and CEO
US Chamber of Commerce

PREFACE

More often than not, companies get into trouble because of ineffective management decisions, not because of lack of expertise. Most books about management don't offer a concrete way to learn how to make more-effective management decisions. Perhaps that's because not too many of them were written by CEOs with effective leadership track records.

The more I thought about the management books in the marketplace, the more I realized the necessity of a different kind of book—a book that would show actual business situations from the perspective of the top leader of an organization. In the fast-paced, change-on-a-dime twenty-first-century business world, these kinds of insights are not just helpful, they're essential.

I wrote this book with all that in mind, first and foremost desiring to help management professionals improve their day-to-day effectiveness and leadership by giving them a CEO's perspective. Thank you for joining me on this journey toward success—as a businessperson, a manager, and a leader.

—MR

(**NOTE:** *For more information on AGCO Corporation, please read the company history at the end of this book and/or visit the AGCO website, www .agcocorp.com.*)

INTRODUCTION

As touched on in the preface, most books on management focus more on principles than actual business-world situations. This limits the effectiveness of such books, as they do not provide much that we can apply to actual business challenges. Success as a manager quite simply requires *doing,* and reading cannot translate to doing without useful examples from the real world of business.

We will certainly discuss management principles, but the core intention of this book is to share the wisdom of an actual CEO by providing true-to-life business scenarios and then analyzing the most effective responses to the challenges portrayed.

Accordingly, we will discuss the things effective managers should and should not do. For example, managers should conclude that they essentially contribute to increased productivity and profitability by focusing on their managerial tasks and delegating other responsibilities and tasks to the appropriate support staff. Managers who are unable to manage because they spend too much time performing other tasks impede productivity. If they impede productivity, they cannot increase profitability. In business, nothing trumps the bottom line.

Whether the root of the problem is lack of clear communication from executive management to middle management, or simply a less-than-optimal management style, this book offers the tools and techniques every manager needs in order to be effective. These tools and techniques make up what we can call the "management tool kit."

The Management Tool Kit

- Management Principles (Essence of Management)
- Strategic Planning and Goal Setting
- Organizational Structure
- Governance and Controls
- Employee Development and Advancement
- Communication
- Motivation

The book is designed to be as useful as possible, a go-to resource to turn to time and time again. Focusing on one element from the management tool kit listed above, each chapter follows the same basic setup:

- opening core statement related to the chapter's main topic (these are words of wisdom I have come to rely on throughout my career)
- succinct and useful definition of the chapter's main topic
- true-to-life business scenario illustrating the truth of the core statement in action
- a few key principles essential to the chapter's topic
- closing how-to for applying the chapter's practical wisdom in day-to-day situations

Once you have read the book, the rest is "simply management"! Join me on the journey to becoming a more-effective manager.

1

THE ESSENCE OF MANAGEMENT

Managers provide an essential contribution to productivity as they focus on managerial tasks and delegate expert responsibilities.

Definition of Management

In order to understand what it means to be an effective manager, we need a practical, useful definition of the term *management.* In simplest terms, management means "causing employees to achieve goals."

In other words, managers do anything necessary to ensure that their organizations (employees) achieve certain goals. This means determining who is responsible for what, when, how, and by what means. Effective management involves active and competent use of all the techniques in the management tool kit: management principles (essence of management); goal setting and strategic planning; organizational structure; governance and controls; employee development and advancement; communication; and motivation. This use of the management tool kit allows managers to *delegate,* which means they assign expert (specialist) tasks to appropriately developed employees, freeing up their own time for management tasks. (See Introduction for management tool kit.)

Mastering all this is essential to success as a manager. Remember, managers provide their most essential contribution to productivity by focusing on managerial tasks and delegating expert responsibilities. Let's look at a true-to-life business scenario to see this truth in action.

True-to-Life Business Scenario: Focusing on Managerial Tasks by Delegating Expert Responsibilities

Amanda is the department manager of a sales function within a medium-size corporation. One of her employees, Brent, has been her direct report for two years. She has provided him with adequate employee development, and he has proved to be a talented salesperson and valued employee. Another employee, Caitlin, has a lot of promise but insufficient experience in sales calls. Amanda recognizes Caitlin's talents, knows she and Brent interact well, and sees an opportunity for further development of both employees at the same time.

Amanda therefore makes the (management) decision to provide further training to Caitlin, who lacks expertise in sales calls, by instructing Brent, the experienced salesperson, to accompany Caitlin to eight sales calls during the following month, to analyze the respective outcomes of each call, and to propose suitable measures for the future.

Amanda, not Brent, is developing Caitlin. This is development as a managerial task. Accompanying Caitlin to her sales conversations and providing the subsequent analysis become expert tasks for Brent, as delegated to him by Amanda. Amanda is developing Caitlin by making the necessary decisions for this purpose; Brent is helping Amanda to achieve these goals by carrying out the required partial tasks she has assigned by means of her authority as manager. (Amanda is, in essence, also further developing Brent through the assignment.)

At the end of the month, Amanda will assess the results (management task) and then make new (management) decisions with respect to Caitlin (and Brent, if applicable). Clearly, Amanda follows the principle of focusing on management tasks by delegating expert responsibilities. This enables her to fulfill her own management responsibility of enhancing productivity and profitability for the company.

Management Control Loop

Depicting management as a control loop (see figure 1-1) can help us efficiently view all relevant management tools and put them into appropriate context.

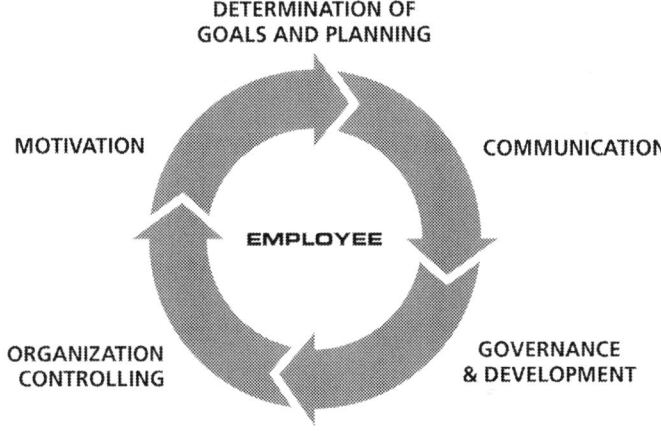

Figure 1-1: Management Control Loop

Basically, the management control loop shows us two things:

1. The necessity for managers to effectively use every element in the management tool kit
2. The ways in which that use (effective or ineffective) impacts employees

In order for the management control loop to work, the company must effectively establish and use organizational structure. Organizational structure primarily includes responsibility for results and decision-making power, both the fundamental roles of effective management. When employees are sure of the chain of command and the line of decision-making authority, it is easier for them to take direction and then achieve set goals. This leads us to goal setting and strategic planning, both of which are key to productivity and profitability, as companies cannot achieve outcomes when management does not adequately use these tools. Employee development, governance, and controls are tools managers need to use to measure the success of goals and plans. Finally, communication and motivation are the tools that make it all work. (We will discuss each of these techniques from the management tool kit in detail throughout the subsequent chapters of this book.)

We can measure the value of any management tool/technique by its influence on employees.

No single management technique is applicable or inapplicable to all employees. The crucial criterion for selecting the appropriate management tool to use in any given situation is the intended effect the manager wants that tool to have on employees. Intention is everything. Effective managers always remain mindful of their desired intentions, as this is the best way to achieve desired results.

Expert versus Management Tasks

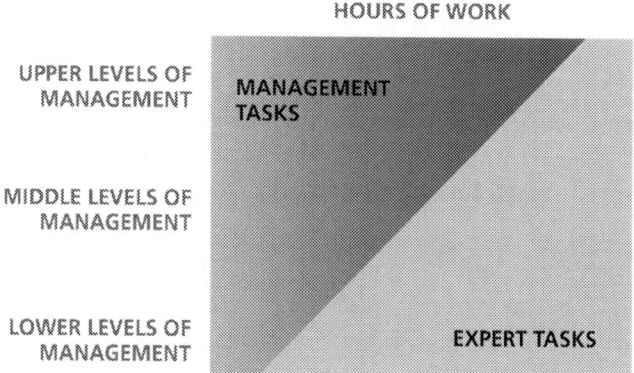

Figure 1-2: Balance between Management Tasks and Expert Tasks

All managers in all three levels of management (upper, middle, and lower) have two types of responsibility: management tasks and expert tasks. Accordingly, during a certain percentage of their working hours, managers engage in management tasks, and during the remaining percentage they engage in expert tasks. But remember, managers' essential contribution to productivity must always involve focusing on managerial tasks and delegating expert responsibilities. Let's look at how to best balance management and expert tasks, following figure 1-2, above.

Balance of Time Distribution between Management Tasks and Expert Tasks

It is key to ensure that there is a balance between management and expert tasks, with neither too much nor too little time spent on one or the other. Figures 1-3 and 1-4 illustrate the pitfalls of a lack of balance of time distribution between expert tasks and management tasks. Although the true-to-life business scenario earlier in this chapter did not illustrate all of Amanda's daily tasks, it did display her effective use of delegating in order to maximize her managerial tasks and minimize her expert ones. We can reasonably surmise that she likely competently achieves this balance in her day-to-day management.

In theory, it seems logical that the share of management tasks should increase at each successive level of management. However, in day-to-day practice, managers—particularly new managers—find allocating more time to management tasks difficult (see figure 1-3). This difficulty primarily occurs when managers do not receive adequate development and so are not sure of how to "let go" of doing all the expert tasks they excelled at in their chosen fields. Whether they are engineers, software developers, salespeople, marketers, procurement specialists, accountants, etc., most new managers receive their promotions based on success in their respective expert activities. However, this success as an expert does not automatically translate to success as a manager! In fact, without adequate management training and development, these promotions often result in the loss of a superb expert and the gain of a bad manager. Specifically, this insufficient training results in the challenge of achieving balance between managerial and expert tasks (especially early on in a manager's career). Promotion without adequate preparation has never created a good manager and never will.

What's the solution? First, employees should be rewarded for excellent performance, but they should not be promoted to management without adequate training. Second, promotion should never be a solution to inadequate managerial staffing or inappropriate managerial workloads. Expert tasks need to be shared fairly and appropriately, and when that becomes impossible, it is management's responsibility to fix the problem in the way that is best for all employees and for the company as a whole.

Remember, always focus on managerial tasks first—that is how we managers best serve the company.

Our core principle highlighted above notwithstanding, many managers do not effectively reduce their expert tasks, whether because of inadequate management development, inability to delegate, or some other reason. Figure 1-3 below shows the typical ratio of management-to-expert tasks.

LESS-EFFECTIVE TIME DISTRIBUTION

MANAGEMENT TASKS

EXPERT TASKS

Figure 1-3: Less-Effective Time Distribution between Management and Expert Tasks

The plain truth is that we often place too much emphasis on expert decisions, particularly in the middle levels of management. The reason for this may be that upper management levels exert strong pressure on the middle levels by expecting them to be knowledgeable in every detail of their field so that they can provide such information to executives, serving as a sort of "buffer zone." Or lower-level managers may depend too much on employee support in expert fields (another instance of the "buffer zone"). Once again, the best way to avoid this issue is by focusing on management tasks.

Any expert promoted to the management level faces a crucial decision and must honestly answer this question: *Am I ready to abandon part of my previous activities?* This "sacrifice" may be difficult because new managers are often promoted to the management level as a result of their professional success as an expert, as we previously described.

Hardworking, dedicated employees will naturally wish to advance, and they will also naturally appreciate the company's validation of their efforts. However, without requisite training, the "reward" quickly becomes a "punishment" as unprepared new managers usually fail dismally—or so overwork themselves to avoid failing that they wind up exhausted, burned out, and miserable, and these quickly lead to ineffective managing, even among the most well-intentioned, dedicated employees, who are usually also the hardest workers. It is management's responsibility to train staff prior to delegating. Staff success means management success; success for one and all means success for the company.

Again, losing sight of the number-one priority of every manager—focusing on managerial tasks—leads to the less-than-ideal situations depicted in figures 1-3 and 1-4. In truth, expert tasks should decrease at the same rate as management tasks increase. However, in addition to the reasons already described, many managers do not accept this fact and believe they should, and can, maintain their previous expert responsibilities. Because of inadequate management development, they believe their departments will be successful only if they themselves control all the tasks. This is clearly a misguided perspective, as delegating is a key management tool. In addition, this attitude leads to chronic work overload, burnout, and many of the other negative results described above. In most cases, managers have themselves to blame because they fail to set clear priorities and neglect to focus on management tasks, resulting in work hours increased by as much as 30 percent.

Not to restate the obvious, but more often than not, overworked managers have received insufficient management development in one or more ways: promoted to management without requisite training; required to carry out too many management tasks and expert tasks simultaneously; or received little to no communication from higher levels of management as to the company's expectations of managers' day-to-day activities.

TOO MUCH FOCUS PLACED ON EXPERT TASKS

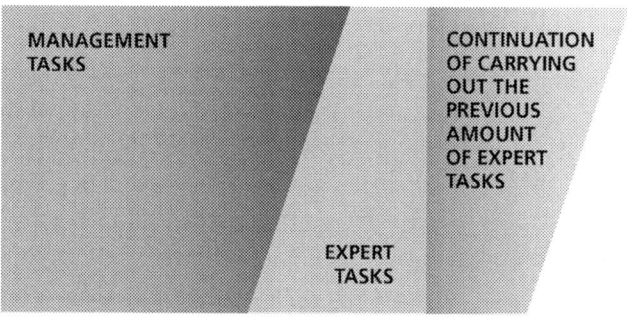

Figure 1-4: Too Much Focus Placed on Expert Tasks

Short-term excessive work hours may be required in certain circumstances (illness, holidays, unexpected events, etc.).

Managers who continue to carry out expert tasks as a habit frequently overestimate themselves as "great experts." They retain decision making for themselves, believing no one else can make decisions as well as they do. Alternatively, upper management fails to effectively communicate expectations to the rest of the management chain. Lower- or midlevel managers whose "hands are tied," requiring them to fulfill expert tasks *and* management tasks, will never be effective managers. Regardless of the underlying reasons, many managers do not act like managers because they do not think like managers.

To be effective and successful, every manager must act *and* think like a manager 100 percent of the time. That means focusing on managerial tasks and delegating expert ones.

Remembering that being a manager is a profession separate from the previous expert position held makes it easier to accept and move past this challenge. Employees who truly enjoy their expert positions should be offered other avenues for reward and promotion so that management is not the only advancement path they can pursue. The management path combines natural ability, professional skill, and earned recognition, creating a win-win for employees, management, and the company. Perhaps the twenty-first century, with all its advances in technology and virtual work environments, will be the one to make this ideal situation a reality in every company.

Management Styles

Theories on psychology and personality abound, and a comprehensive discussion of them would be beyond the scope of this book. However, effective management does entail an understanding of people and human dynamics, so we must briefly describe some personality basics as they pertain to management styles. There are many useful personality-type paradigms and sorters, but most require an entire book or course training to adequately explain them. (Myers-Briggs Type Indicator [MBTI], Keirsey Personality Sorter, and McCrae/Costa "Big Five" are but a few of the more worthwhile ones to investigate.[1])

For managers, however, Everything DiSC can be more effective in day-to-day use. DiSC stands for *dominance, influence, steadiness,* and *conscientiousness,* each of which is an area that individual people most identify with in behavior and relationships. The Everything DiSC model correlates each of these main four areas into specific key segments of workplace behaviors: accuracy,

---

[1]   Isabel Briggs Myers with Peter B. Myers, *Gifts Differing: Understanding Personality Type* (Mountain View, CA: CCP, Inc., 1980, 1995); David Keirsey, *Please Understand Me II* (Del Mar, CA: Prometheus Nemesis Book Company, 1998); R. R. McCrae and P. T. Costa, "Reinterpreting the Myers-Briggs Type Indicator from the Perspective of the Five-Factor Model of Personality," *Journal of Personality* 57, no. 1 (1989): 17–40, doi:10.1111/j.1467-6494.1989.tb00759.x.

action, challenges, collaboration, enthusiasm, results, support, and stability.[2] Most individuals will display strengths in at least three key segments, which means they will display weaknesses or limitations in the other segments. That helps us see that managers benefit from having at least a working understanding of how different personality types behave, react, and respond. Effective managers can and do benefit from achieving such understanding, and it enables them to adapt their management styles as needed.

Let's remain aware that personality traits can have positive and negative expressions. Assertiveness and attention to detail each have an appropriate place in different workplace situations, as do enthusiasm and accommodation; however, if any of them are taken to an extreme, they can create less-than-ideal situations. Suffice it to say that the infinite combinations of personalities make life interesting indeed. Consequently, they can make day-to-day interaction in the workplace rather challenging. Keeping all this in mind allows for more-effective daily management of employees, more-successful interaction with upper management, and optimal performance within the company.

A final word of caution: use awareness of personality types as a general guide to what makes people tick. That is, our knowledge here should ideally be a tool that enhances our instincts and intuition about the employees we manage (as well as our peers and superiors). Avoid using and thinking about people in terms of buzzwords, as such popular psychology jargon is often overused and misused. The goal here is not to be judgmental, just to be aware.

Everyone has strengths, weaknesses, and limitations. As managers, we must balance our interactions with wisdom, fairness, and understanding. So now let's move on to the daily situations where personality and management style blend.

Situational Management

Managers can approach the primary management objective of "causing employees to achieve goals" in different ways. However, the issue of

---

[2]   Inscape Publishing, *Everything DiSC* (Minneapolis: Inscape Publishing, 2007–12).

appropriate management behavior does arise. Over the years, management theorists have developed a range of models that serve to explain management behavior. Let's explore these models in order to better understand management behavior.

One common model describes two behavioral extremes: the authoritarian management style and the cooperative management style. According to this model, managers must select from two vastly different behaviors—in fact, they are polar opposites. Although authoritarian management was the style of choice for decades, the recommended style of choice in today's business world is cooperative management. As we have already seen—and will continue to see as our discussion progresses—the twenty-first-century workplace entails cooperation as part of success, from both the employee and management perspective. Authoritarian managers will generally not succeed when 50 percent or more of the workforce telecommutes, and employees who do not buy in to cooperative efforts (i.e., teamwork) will generally not succeed in today's competitive workplace.

All that said, however, we must keep in mind that any worthwhile concept of management must be based on knowing there is no ideal management style that will be equally effective in all situations. This common-sense truth applies to life in general: knowing that different ideas and approaches work at different times is quite simply what we call "wisdom." Thus, different management styles may be appropriate at different times, depending on any or all of the following variables: employee requirements, supervisors, colleagues, customers, and the specific issue at hand. Managers should never restrict themselves to the exclusive application of one or the other extreme of management styles. That is not effective leadership. Effective management and good leadership should be situational (i.e., they should correspond to the demands associated with the actual current situation). Effective managers can and will always adapt their style to fit the needs of the moment.

To a certain extent, every decision and all behavior displayed by a manager is

1. focused on fulfilling a certain task and
2. influenced by relationships with other people.

In addition, every management decision—and, generally speaking, any behavior displayed by a manager—contains a certain degree of both task orientation (TO) and relationship orientation (RO).

Task and Relationship Orientation

Task Orientation (TO)

Task orientation (TO) is the extent to which the manager actively makes decisions and directs employee performance. The primary characteristics of TO management are *initiating, organizing,* and *instructing.*

Relationship Orientation (RO)

Relationship orientation (RO) is the extent to which the manager maintains personal work relationships. The primary characteristics of RO management are *listening, encouraging,* and *building trust.*

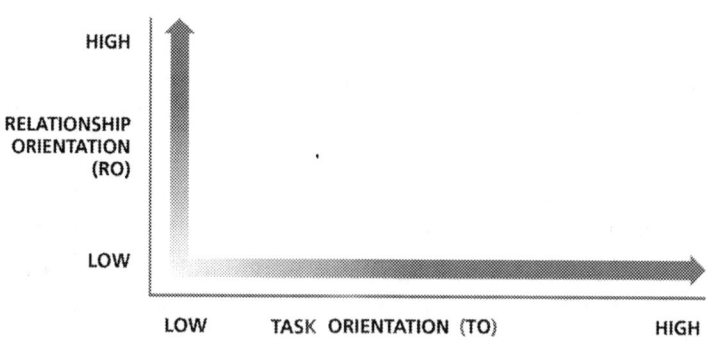

TASK AND RELATIONSHIP ORIENTATION

Figure 1-5: Task and Relationship Orientation

RO and TO can be effective or ineffective, depending on the individual manager. Specifically, it is the *way* in which a manager uses TO and/or RO that makes it effective or ineffective. Every circumstance is different, and it is an individual choice when a manager uses TO or RO. The key point to remember is this: always opting for one style limits effective management and successful leadership.

So now let's turn our attention to the actual styles of management, as based on TO and RO.

Basic Styles of Management Behavior

Now let's bring our discussion of preferences of RO, TO, or a combination of the two to include the DiSC model referred to earlier. Recall the key areas of workplace behaviors: accuracy, action, challenges, collaboration, enthusiasm, results, support, and stability. As indicated in the descriptions of RO and TO, it's easy to see that managers whose strengths lie in the areas of action, challenges, and results will prefer using TO; conversely, managers whose strengths lie in the areas of collaboration, support, and stability will prefer RO. What complicates things is the way in which employees respond to the managers' preferences, the extent of their development, etc. Remember, all individuals—employees and managers alike—will display strengths, weaknesses, and limitations in various areas. Again, remember that the mark of an effective manager is the ability to adapt management style to the situation at hand.

Management Styles in Daily Situations

Simply stated, managers who take an RO approach exhibit a *relationship style* of management, managers who take a TO approach exhibit a *task style,* and managers who combine RO and TO in their approach exhibit an *integrated style.*

Using the Relationship, Task, and Integrated Styles

Different situations present different challenges for the manager, depending on the management style used. Thus, the application of every basic style may either be suitable or unsuitable to the situation (depending upon the situational requirements). Remember that because very few situations requiring managerial decisions are identical, there is no ideal management behavior equally suitable to all requirements. It will be extremely helpful to improve the following abilities: a feeling for the situation, consciousness of style, and scope of style. Understanding the situation relates to the manager's ability to recognize certain demands directed to him or her by supervisors, colleagues, or employees. Prejudices, bias, lack of empathy, and lack of experience often obstruct a manager's ability to recognize what others truly expect of him or her. Scope of style is the manager's ability to change the basic style, which can be more, or less, effective. Again, remember that adapting management style to the situation at hand is key to managerial effectiveness and success.

Applying What You Have Learned

Following the core statement that opened this chapter, our mission as managers, first and foremost, is always to contribute to company productivity by focusing on managerial tasks and delegating expert responsibilities. In order to accomplish that, we must do the following:

1. Utilize the management control loop (the mechanism for using all the elements of the management tool kit).
2. Establish a balance between expert tasks and management tasks.
3. Recognize our management style and adapt it as needed.

By incorporating the above items into our daily routine, we are well on the way to becoming effective managers. And that's "simply management"!

Now that we have discussed the essence of management—management control loop, expert versus management tasks, and management styles—let's move on to a deeper discussion of how and when to use each element of the management tool kit to optimal effect.

2

STRATEGIC PLANNING AND GOAL SETTING

Strategic planning and goal setting should always be a group process.

Definition of Strategic Planning and Goal Setting

A *goal* is a declaration of intent to reach a desirable future result at a defined point. *Goal setting* is the system of directing efforts and resources for the purpose of achieving a desired outcome. *Strategic planning* is the establishment of objectives and the formulation, evaluation, and selection of the policies, strategies, methods, and actions required to achieve those objectives. Such planning can be short- or long-term, as determined by management.

Goals should help the company make the most of its *potential* opportunities. Therefore, strategic planning and goal setting are management tools used to achieve company objectives. We can think of plans and goals as steps we must take in order to accomplish desired objectives. This is precisely why strategic planning and goal setting should always be a group process. There is always a greater probability of achieving desired objectives when everyone is involved and engaged in the process. In addition, today's globalization and telecommuting have made this more critical than ever.

Let's further explore the key management tools of strategic planning and goal setting.

True-to-Life Business Scenario: Strategic Planning and Goal Setting as a Group Process

In any organization, the key to achieving successful goals lies in aligning them with the overall business strategy. To that end, goal setting must start at the top, with senior leadership. That is the only way to effectively ensure alignment.

One approach that can be quite successful in aligning goals is leveraging an annual strategic-planning process. Let's use AGCO as an example. The global strategy and integration team holds a two-day global leadership summit. The purpose of the summit is to develop the organization's five-year global strategic initiatives and the annual goals that will support those initiatives.

For example, one goal may be to run a more efficient global organization. In concert with this goal, the leadership team may also develop a goal/target to reduce spending by 10 percent. Both goals are then cascaded (as appropriate) throughout the organization. These goals could appear to conflict with one another—that is, becoming more efficient may require some additional funding—yet the organization is being asked to reduce costs at the same time. Consequently, communication will be key to keeping the business aligned: each function and region must move in the same direction and strive to achieve the same targets.

How might specific departments or regions align with these goals and, at the same time, ensure alignment with both global goals?

One area that would align with the goal of reducing spending is the global purchasing function. In order to meet this goal, they establish a specific functional goal: reducing the number of steel vendors so the company will be able to take advantage of volume-based discounts. The expectation is that this will enable the company to realize a 20 percent price reduction for steel.

But what about the efficiency goal? How can purchasing align with this goal? The global purchasing leadership team creatively considers how to set a goal for efficiency while simultaneously reducing spending. The consensus is to leverage supplier diversity, which will offer increased innovation without increasing costs.

Each region must also align with and set goals based on the global goals. Let's consider that the South American region would like to increase sales by 10 percent. The region must consider the global goal to reduce spending while at the same time increase sales. If the region decides to spend more money on marketing to increase sales, they will also have to develop specific goals around reducing costs. The goals continue to cascade through to each employee, who will have a performance goal that supports the global and regional goals.

That brings us to the next point: How does a matrix organization affect the goal-setting process? In a matrix organization, an employee will report to a manager in the region; at the same time, he or she will have a matrix-reporting relationship with a manager in the function. When the manager and the matrix manager communicate, this is an ideal situation. When they don't communicate, it can result in competing (and often conflicting) goals for the employee.

This further illustrates why it is so critical for strategic planning and goal setting to be a group process. Once the manager and the matrix manager both understand and mutually agree upon the plans and goals, they can communicate a consensus to the employee. This makes employee buy-in much easier to achieve—and the success of the plans and goals much more likely, as everyone at every level within the company feels equally invested in that success.

Strategic Planning Tools

As management tools, goal setting and strategic planning serve to establish a formal decision-making process by systematically addressing the following:

STRATEGIC PLANNING TOOLS

KEY QUESTION/CHALLENGE	KEY SOLUTION METHOD USED
WHERE DO WE STAND?	SITUATION ANALYSIS (OF PAST AND PRESENT)
WHERE DO WE WANT TO GO?	SETTING GOALS (DETERMINATION OF DESIRED OUTCOME)
HOW DO WE GET THERE?	PLANNING (INCLUDING OPERATIONAL PLANNING [PROCESS] AND FINANCIAL PLANNING [BUDGET])

As the table above reflects, goal setting and strategic planning entail a continuous process. This process involves specifying target conditions against which we can measure the actual development. Furthermore, the measures implemented should allow us to bring the actual state as close to the target as possible. Goal setting and planning provide the means for deciding what employees must achieve this week, this month, and/or this year in order for the company to thrive during the next month, the next year, over the subsequent five years, and throughout whatever short- and/ or long-term time frames management sets.

We must keep in mind that goals are about the future; we have to plan for them in the present if we want to make them reality—otherwise, they'll never be more than unrealized dreams. Goals and dreams are not one and the same. We achieve our goals by planning properly. There are no shortcuts.

To illustrate this, let's look at the past. If the residents of a fortified city in the year 1700 had considered what they believed their city would look like in the year 2000, they might have imagined that the fortification of the city would have doubled, and that the city walls would be indestructible and able to withstand attacks from any type of artillery. That would have been a sound conclusion, based on eighteenth-century technology. Twentieth-century technology made that conclusion obsolete, just as the ever-evolving technology of the twenty-first century makes that of the twentieth equally obsolete. We cannot even imagine what breakthroughs future centuries will develop. This is the realm of the visionaries and the entrepreneurs. Yes, such individuals need to have imagination, dreams, and enthusiasm, but without a management team in place to ensure effective goal setting and planning, none of those things will ever be part of reality for any company.

Simply put, goal setting and planning must take place in the present but look toward the future. This is the best way for management to ensure the coordination of individual goals while simultaneously designing the most effective and most creative planning process.

The most important things to remember are these: Strategic planning and goal setting do not refer to future decisions but to the *future impact of today's decisions*. As such, strategic planning and goal setting should always be a *group process*.

Establishing a Goal-Setting and Strategic-Planning Process

The table below (which expands on the table at the beginning of this chapter) offers an effective model to use for establishing a goal-setting and strategic-planning process. Clearly, managers across industries can apply this model to their own organizations' goal-setting and strategic-planning process with a great degree of effectiveness, as has been the case throughout many companies over time.

GOAL-SETTING AND STRATEGIC-PLANNING PROCESS MODEL

WHERE DO WE STAND?
CORPORATE IDEALS (MISSION AND VISION)
COMPANY OBJECTIVES (BUSINESS ACTIVITIES/OPERATIONS)
COMPETING LANDSCAPE ANALYSIS (ASSESSING THE EXTERNAL ENVIRONMENT)
ANALYSIS OF STRENGTHS AND WEAKNESSES
WHERE DO WE WANT TO GO?
WHERE DO WE WANT TO GO?
ASSUMPTIONS (WHAT WE ALREADY KNOW)
GOALS (WHAT WE WANT TO ACHIEVE)
HOW DO WE GET THERE?
GUIDELINES (WHAT WE CAN REASONABLY ATTAIN)
BUDGETS (FISCAL RESPONSIBILITY OF WHAT WE CAN AFFORD)

Using the table above, let's examine each component of the process. A thorough understanding of every one of these components will lead to a competent implementation of an effective company process for goal setting and strategic planning.

Where Do We Stand?

Corporate Ideals: Mission and Vision

Corporate ideals are declarations of intent based on standards established by corporate management. The company mission and vision define the character of corporate activities.

Company Objectives

The *objective* is the company's general scope of activities. Although company objectives may frequently be used synonymously with corporate goals, our discussion of company objectives will center on business activities—that is, daily operations whose effectiveness we can measure and quantify. When we refer to corporate goals, we are not necessarily considering measurable objectives. For our purposes here, the definition of *objective* must be neither too loose nor too restrictive. Objectives should also accurately describe a company's active market. Finally, objectives should refer to today, not to the past or to a (desirable) future situation. A good rule of thumb is that if management and employees have trouble stating the objective in a single sentence, chances are customers will too.

The objective of the company should describe the common denominator of all corporate activities.

Competing Landscape Analysis

It is essential to assess the external environment (i.e., the company's competitors). Managers must accordingly clarify and evaluate the most important external factors affecting the company, expressing those factors in a measurable/quantifiable form (or at least a form that is as measurable/quantifiable as possible).

Analysis of Strengths and Weaknesses

Strengths and weaknesses are simply a company's advantages and disadvantages, as compared with those of other companies. There are no absolute strengths or weaknesses; they only result from comparison with other companies.

Profit and Product Assessment

Profit potential is the business area in which the company sees the opportunity to achieve successes and generate profits. It consists of a precisely defined market and an offer that satisfies the corresponding demands and requirements (product/service in the market).

Product portfolio is an evaluation system that illustrates the position and size of profit potentials. It is defined by market type and quality on the one hand and the company's position within the market on the other.

Where Do We Want to Go?

Assumptions: What We Already Know, in Quantifiable Terms

An *assumption* is the assessment of a development trend that is outside one's own area of influence and is based on a certain point in time. Therefore, an assumption is not a forecast, a measure, or a goal.

Assumptions should always be based on a time frame or a point in time and should be as measurable as possible (including quantities, diagrams, tables, etc.).

Because goals should be geared toward the future and can only be derived from the past to a limited degree, the compilation of assumptions is a key requirement for establishing goals and making decisions on how to reach them. As long as assumptions do not change, the goals will remain unchanged as well. Should the established assumptions prove to be incorrect, management must initiate a new planning process, which leads to newly defined goals or modified procedures and priorities.

When compiling assumptions, we often wonder about the likelihood of their actually coming to fruition. As important as this may be, it is of secondary priority because the main purpose of establishing assumptions is not making prophetical statements but finding a basis for the determination of goals. In other words, we should only compile assumptions relating to developments with a direct influence on the company's future.

Goals: What We Want to Achieve, in Quantifiable Terms

Remember, *goals* are steps toward desired outcomes. The goal-setting and strategic-planning process is the pivotal point of twenty-first-century management—especially when conducted as a group process. All other management technologies and measures are based on agreed-upon goals.

How Do We Get There?

Guidelines

Guidelines are general conditions that reflect the corporate policy. They should serve as directives for individual employees, with respect to results, responsibility, and decision-making authority. Management often summarizes all this in an organizational and/or a policies-and-procedures manual that includes guidelines for the company as a whole and for individual divisions/departments. Guidelines can refer to any corporate function (e.g., pricing, quality, investments, profit utilization, procurement, marketing, personnel/HR, etc.), and they should always be expressed in a measurable manner.

In addition, management uses guidelines to specify in more detail the company mission and vision, its valued expectations, and its intended purpose for individual organizational departments. Finally, guidelines control the achievement of goals. Thus, we can turn to our guidelines when asking, "How do we get there?" Effective guidelines will help us determine what we can reasonably expect to attain.

Budgets

Budgets are measurements expressed in monetary terms. They represent goals and responsibilities to be achieved within specific time frames. Budgets are the "pricing tables" in planning, and they create clear points for governance and controls. The creation of a budget without previous establishment of a goal-setting and strategic-planning process is a game of numbers, not professional management.

Every management triangle (see "Triangle Principle" in chapter 3) should have a budget and should have participated in the budget's creation. Budgets should cascade appropriately throughout the organization, reaching down as far as possible. In corporate practice, we often encounter the erroneous notion that only upper-management levels should develop budgets. This is simply not so. Budgets should include all objectives put forth in the goal-setting and strategic-planning process. They should also include all organization areas. Budgets should include not only cost amounts but sales numbers and profit margins.

Budgets must be compatible with the organization; that is, the budget system should reflect every management triangle, and every management team should have a budget that reflects the overall system. If the organization changes, the budget system must be adjusted accordingly.

Budget consolidation creates more disadvantages than advantages. This refers to the inclusion of budget values in other budgets, which is rarely, if ever, worthwhile.

We can summarize the importance of budgets concisely and in simple terms: budgets reflect fiscal responsibility by enabling us to determine what we can afford and helping us set the financial aspect of the goal-setting and strategic-planning process. This is why they are so critical to governance and controls.

Planning Techniques: How Do We Get There from Here?

Having thoroughly explored the importance of answering the key questions of effective goal setting and strategic planning—"Where do we stand?," "Where do we want to go?," and "How do we get there?"—we must now turn our attention to actual planning techniques. In essence, these techniques provide us with options for how to get from *here* (where we are) to *there* (where we want to be).

We've already seen that various measures are necessary in order to achieve goals. It makes sense to determine them within the context of an informal exchange of ideas, and then to write them all up—regardless of seeming importance and interdependencies. Next, we can classify and categorize them by topic, chronology, etc. Various planning techniques are available for this (e.g., charts, tables, matrices, etc.). When it's necessary to clearly represent chronological and functional dependencies, choose a method that reflects these measures. Before the measures are represented graphically, determine the requisite data: responsibilities, time requirements in hours or days, costs of individual measures, and so forth.

Three questions facilitate planning in practice:

1. Is the time needed realistic and in agreement with the goals?
2. Are the costs realistic and in agreement with the goals?
3. Can we meet the determined deadline?

Given the wide array of Internet downloads and software applications available, it's relatively easy to plug in the time frames and other pertinent variables and then choose the graphical representation desired for output. What is crucial here is ensuring the accuracy of all data input, as well as determining that all time frames and goals are attainable, of course.

Finally, most important of all is ensuring that the planning techniques used foster collaboration—remember, it's always more effective when planning is a group process.

The Manager's Role

In general, goals are measurable (quantifiable) results that managers and employees are trying to achieve. This not only includes innovative results but also routine goals. Management determines the time frames (short term, long term, etc.) for all goals.

Goals should be within the scope of the objective of the company, derived from strengths and weaknesses, and based on assumptions. Goals should not be a mere continuation of the past; they should be derived from an evaluation of the future (assumptions). To reemphasize our earlier description, goals reflect the future impact of today's planning. Finally and crucially, goals should always be set during a group process.

Now that we've explored why goal setting and strategic planning are so important, and how to establish an effective system and process for them, let's explore some of the most common obstacles encountered as part of the process of strategic planning and goal setting.

The Most Common Obstacles to Goal Setting and Strategic Planning

First, we need to determine some key characteristics of goals. Goals should be **SMART**: **s**pecific, **m**easurable, **a**chievable, **r**elevant, and **t**ime-driven.

- **Specific:** Goals should define precise priorities that are linked to broader business objectives.
- **Measurable:** Goals should be quantifiable, providing a metric for successful accomplishment.
- **Achievable:** Goals should represent an ambitious yet reasonably attainable target.
- **Relevant:** Goals should be under the individual's control and within his or her span of authority.
- **Time-driven:** The time frame for achieving goals should be within a one-year period.

It is up to the manager to ensure that all goals are SMART, that all goals align with company objectives (cascaded clearly and efficiently, as appropriate), and that goal setting is always a group process. However, even when managers do all this, obstacles to attaining set goals abound. Typical obstacles include but are not limited to lack of time, old habits ("dying hard"), and fear of change. These are challenging but not insurmountable. Managers must overcome such obstacles. Effective managers always do.

Another obstacle that pertains more to upper management is that we tend to design plans for times of economic lows, while we bask in the euphoria of economic booms. To be blunt, this is a practice doomed to fail. It is very difficult to assess the future appropriately if we use the past as a benchmark. We must work with new standards in order to make the process of goal setting and strategic planning innovative and effective. Here again we can see how imperative it is to make this a group process, as innovation is usually a product of teamwork and brainstorming.

All that said, we must always remember that our objective is to plan today for tomorrow's success. Sweeping changes (economic, technological, and so forth) are often unforeseen and usually unavoidable, but that does not excuse lack of planning.

It's useful to remember that nothing can foster workplace commonality and teamwork like an effective process of goal setting and strategic planning that is established as a cooperative effort, with mutually agreed-upon parameters and completely equitable measures.

Goal Alignment

The true-to-life business scenario at the beginning of this chapter illustrates the importance of goal alignment. The twenty-first-century workplace, with its globalization and telecommuting, has made this more critical than ever. To be sure, the most important information will always exist in the minds of the people involved (such as employees, managers, and executives). The primary objective is to make the knowledge that exists in various departments available to everyone, so that every department, and the company as a whole, will benefit. That is an appropriate cascade, and the most effective way to cultivate it is by *collaborative planning.*

Collaborative Planning

There are several advantages to collaborative planning between managers and employees:

1. The team processes a greater quantity and a higher quality of information.
2. The involvement of all team members and managers increases motivation, commitment, and identification with the tasks; consequently, this facilitates future implementation of planning.
3. The team is capable of performing a greater amount of planning in less time. Therefore, goal setting and planning should always be a group process.
4. Managers should plan in collaboration with employees; that is, managers should not plan for employees.

Collaborative planning fosters teamwork (i.e., cooperation). The key result of the planning process is not the plan itself but the understanding,

agreement, and common action that result from an effective planning process, which should always be a group process.

Let's emphasize that managers should not expect "spectacular" results from the goal-setting and planning process, as the result is often merely a confirmation of previously planned measures. However, the planning process does make these measures binding for everyone, and it simultaneously increases identification with the process. The objective of a goal-setting and planning process that is fully integrated within the company is not so much about achieving the desired numbers as it is about the process itself. Again, the essential aspect of the process is the collaboration of a group of managers in the upper and intermediate management levels who, with input from employees, determine the future of the company in a way that is binding for everyone. Remember, this is a cooperative, collaborative effort. This is why the consensual decision-making method is recommended, as it ensures that everyone involved is backing the established plan. It does not mean that employees have equivalent authority to managers, but it does mean obtaining employee buy-ins is easier because they feel the effort is participatory. Teamwork and collaboration work best when they feel real and honest, when management practices them with integrity and sincerity. Employees can determine when this is and isn't true.

Teamwork is invaluable to every organization; it makes it possible to assess environmental opportunities and risks, as well as corporate strengths and weaknesses, from the point of view of everyone involved. Moreover, it ensures that everyone embraces the objectives and measures established in cooperative discussions and that management will be able to implement these objectives and measures into practical applications, without resistance. (This applies to both day-to-day operations and long-term, overarching desired outcomes.) This system fulfills employees' basic need to contribute, increases their personal commitment to the company, encourages them to share responsibility, and creates a win-win situation for employees, managers, and the company as a whole.

Planning Responsibilities

Goal setting and planning are management tasks, key components of the management tool kit. That said, managers cannot and must not delegate goal setting and planning. Keep in mind that cooperative planning means that employees participate, not that they actually establish goals or plans. Similarly, corporate planning departments cannot and should not make planning decisions on their own without management input and approval. Such departments should only handle the responsibilities listed below.

Planning Department Duties

- organization and implementation of the planning process
- provision of help for individual managers
- coordination of individual plans
- summarization of the budget
- establishment of an overarching plan (i.e., plans and controls)

It is critical that corporate planning departments fulfill their responsibilities, but it is equally critical that they do not overstep their boundaries. Individual managers must have the latitude to plan effectively, and to engage their employees in the collaborative planning process.

Change Management Definition

Change management is the coordination of a structured period of transition (i.e., from situation A to situation B) in order to achieve lasting change within an organization. It can be reactive or proactive, and it can vary in scope from continuous improvement of small ongoing changes to existing processes, to radical and substantial changes that involve organizational strategy. Regardless of its scope and whether it is reactive or proactive, change management usually follows five steps:

1. Recognizing the need for change
2. Clarifying the desired outcome ("where we want to be")
3. Planning how to effect the change

4. Achieving the transition
5. Managing effectively in order to ensure lasting change and resulting success

Such tools/techniques as motivation, communication, and management style are key to achieving lasting change. Employees and management must be unified in order for change management to be successful. Therefore, always communicate such plans to employees, as this will more readily result in buy-in. Change management is an offshoot of strategic planning, and planning must always be a group process.

The Change Management Plan

Most companies expect to experience major changes in terms of market and products within the next few years. This fact alone should be reason enough for a systematic analysis of the goal-setting and planning process. Nevertheless, this type of management tool is still not widely used, even in large companies, although the methods are well-known and have proven track records.

Consider the following ideas, which require a systematic goal-setting and strategic-planning process:

1. We know the future will be different from the past. Of course we don't know exactly how it will be different, but a positive attitude toward new things will help us cope better with the future. Planning backward from the future activates innovative and creative thought processes. That means we must consider the future impact of our present decisions, which is the cornerstone of effective goal setting and planning. Past experience should merely serve as an effective support, providing certain valuable information to our decision making, but the future should always be our prime motivator when setting goals.
2. We know that the sequence of changes will increase; that is, more changes will come about in ever-shorter intervals. For example, it took mankind tens of thousands of years to achieve a speed of 25 miles per hour, but just another 130 years to reach a speed of 25,000

miles per hour. Similarly, the invention of penicillin alone saved more human lives than all previously known medical treatments.

3. Today, there are several evolutionary processes with almost revolutionary character. Rapid technological advances result in significant changes across all industries. This results in increased expectations as to quality of life. People become aware of the advantages of a comfortable lifestyle, and they want to live that lifestyle—*now.* Computers, the Internet, and, most recently, social media and smartphones have completely and permanently changed life as we know it.

4. The consequences of management decisions are becoming more and more short-term, while their costs are increasing. Often, products only have a cycle of a few years in which they can generate a profit. In many areas, the development timetable for new products has become significantly longer and more expensive (e.g., pharmaceutical products). In addition, the increasing complexity of today's decentralized organizations requires an intensive process for goal setting and planning—and with good reason. As a result, managers must work to ensure that decentralized independent divisions stay together and are aligned with the common goal of embracing the company's overarching mission and vision and achieving its desired outcomes.

The foregoing ideas are important to consider and keep in mind. However, bear in mind that establishing and following a workable system and process for goal setting and strategic planning is the best way to successfully deal with change.

As managers, we simply must embrace the inevitable: change. Designing the management system to handle change effectively must be part of every company's goal-setting and strategic-planning process.

Applying What You Have Learned

As the core statement opening this chapter emphasizes, strategic planning and goal setting should always be a group process. We managers must make sure to remember that, and our day-to-day management must reflect it by including employees in the process and encouraging their full engagement and buy-in.

Here are some essential steps related to strategic planning and goal setting that we all need to implement:

1. Utilize the key management tools of strategic planning and goal setting.
2. Ensure goal alignment through appropriate cascade at all levels.
3. Recognize the need for change and implement such changes effectively, ensuring short- and long-term success.

By incorporating the above items 1 through 3 into our daily routine, we are well on the way to becoming effective managers. And that's "simply management"!

Now that we've thoroughly discussed goal setting and strategic planning, let's turn to another key management tool: organizational structure, which we will explore in the next chapter.

3

ORGANIZATIONAL STRUCTURE

Like all management tools, the organization tool is easy to use
but often misunderstood.

Definition of Organizational Structure

When used as a management tool, *organizational structure* is the determination of the allocation of responsibilities necessary to achieve desired results, as well as the determination of the line of authority (chain of command) and decision-making power related to those responsibilities—simply put, who does what and by whose authority.

Companies with a clear organizational structure usually effectively use all the other management tools and techniques. A clear line of authority eliminates a lot of confusion, conflict, and duplication of effort. Nevertheless, as the core statement reflects, although the organizational structure tool is easy to use, it is often misunderstood.

Let's expand our discussion by examining a true-to-life business scenario that utilizes organizational structure with maximum effectiveness.

True-to-Life Business Scenario: Global Matrix Organizational Structure

As the world's largest engine manufacturing company, ACME knows about dispersed project teams in a global organization. Headquartered in Munich, Germany, with nearly fifteen thousand employees in sixty countries, team collaboration and communication are critical to the company's success.

The company has two corporate strategic goals: (1) to increase gross sales by 10 percent and (2) to reduce costs by 5 percent. These goals cascade throughout the organization's regional groups.

Tatiana, SVP for South America, has a goal to increase gross sales by 10 percent within the region. She reports to Suzanne, CEO/President.

Franco, VP of Finance for South America, has a goal to reduce costs by 5 percent within the region. He also reports to Luis, SVP Finance

Arno, VP of Sales and Marketing, reports to Tatiana. He has been working for months to acquire a contract with the largest engine distribution dealer, which will significantly increase sales for South America. For this marketing expenditure, Arno needs purchasing approval from Franco, VP of Finance for South America. As a result of Franco's delay in approving the expenditure, Arno loses the contract to a competitor.

We can clearly see that the silos in this type of management structure can promote conflicting organizational goals that compete against one another (see figure 3-1, below). Management's intention to cascade goals and strategic planning is there, but the company's organizational structure impedes it.

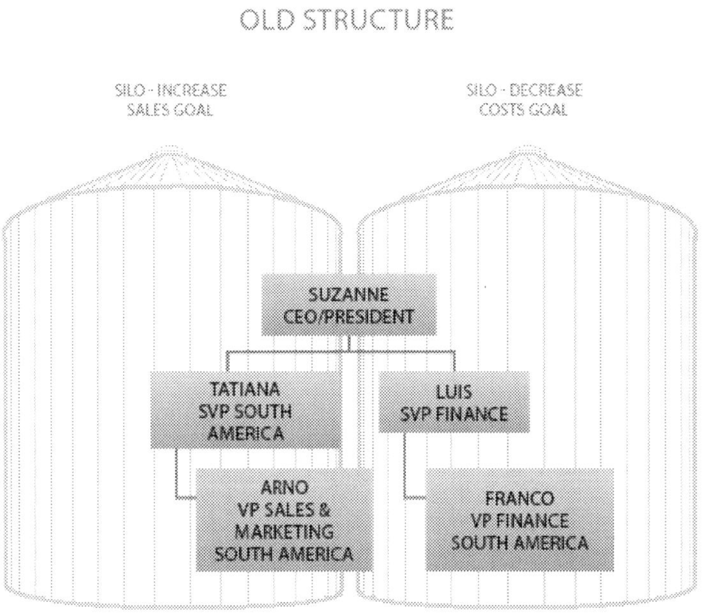

OLD STRUCTURE

SILO - INCREASE
SALES GOAL

SILO - DECREASE
COSTS GOAL

SUZANNE
CEO/PRESIDENT

TATIANA
SVP SOUTH
AMERICA

LUIS
SVP FINANCE

ARNO
VP SALES &
MARKETING
SOUTH AMERICA

FRANCO
VP FINANCE
SOUTH AMERICA

Figure 3-1: Less-Effective Old Structure (Silos)

When Suzanne, CEO/President of ACME, learns of the lost opportunity with the new vendor, she decides to make some changes to the organizational structure in order to remove barriers within the business.

In the new matrix organizational structure (see figure 3-2, below), Franco (VP of Finance for South America) now has a dual reporting structure: a direct report to Tatiana (SVP for South America) and a matrix report to Luis (SVP of Finance). This dual reporting is designed to ensure alignment of regional goals (increase sales by 10 percent) and functional goals (reduce costs by 5 percent). Franco's direct manager is in the South American region so that day-to-day decisions can be effectively accomplished. Franco's strategic manager is located at the corporate headquarters. As in all matrix organizations, it is important for Tatiana and Luis to communicate with each other and with Franco. Clear communication will enable Franco to carry out his responsibilities with maximum effectiveness and without the obstacles of conflicting goals, logistical delays, and other impediments to success.

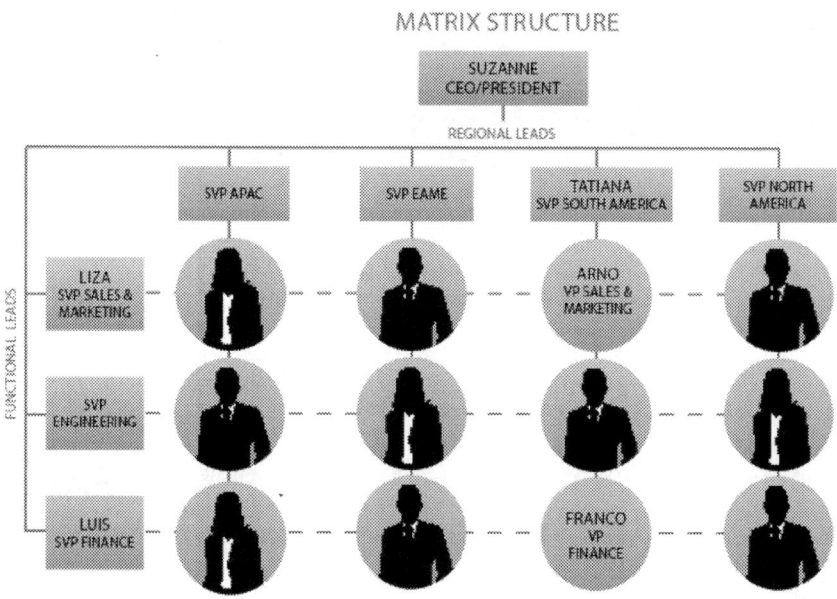

Figure 3-2: More-Effective Matrix Structure

As we can clearly see, the matrix organizational structure allows for the breakdown of silos and the simultaneous support of the business functions' collaboration to drive the company's success. Seeing the potential for across-the-board success that improved organizational structure can have, Suzanne (CEO/President) makes the necessary changes: an effective use of this key management tool.

Improving the organizational structure has the potential to create across-the-board success at any and every company, as the above true-to-life business scenario illustrates. Remember, the organizational structure tool is easy to use but often misunderstood. Let's explore some different types of organizations in order to see why that is the case.

Types of Organizations

Before we can discuss types of organizations, we need to describe some key organizational principles: the *management triangle* and *decentralization/centralization*.

Triangle Principle

A certain number of management (organizational) triangles (see figure 3-3) must be in place in order for a company's organizational structure to be clear and useful.

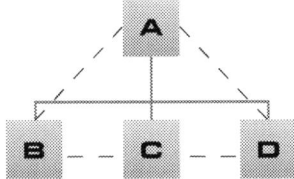

Figure 3-3: Management Triangle

The triangle depicted in figure 3-3 reflects a clear and useful organizational structure that expresses the following:

Results B + Results C + Results D + Management through A = Results of the Management Triangle

Theoretically, it *is* that simple. But remember the core statement that opened this chapter: the organization tool is easy to use but often misunderstood. The next key principle—decentralization/centralization—shows where some of the complications arise.

Decentralization versus Centralization

An organization may be either centralized or decentralized. *Decentralization* means the transfer of responsibility for results and decision-making authority within a precisely defined, general framework to organizational units located as far away from corporate management as possible. That said, decentralization requires effective delegating.

In addition to the requisite use of effective delegating, the success of a decentralized organization depends largely upon the attitude and behavior of the manager(s) involved. Centrally focused managers take on all decisions and problems. They operate based on the premise of: "What I myself did not do here is not done properly." Conversely, decentrally focused managers assume that others (experts on their teams) are far better suited to make certain decisions than they (the managers) are. They operate based on the premise of, "I have sufficiently developed my team, and I trust them to make the necessary decisions and achieve the desired outcomes." Clearly, it is very difficult to anchor decentralized attitudes and behavior within a company. It is particularly difficult in situations where individual department/division managers do not consider the advantages of decentralization. They prefer to make decisions themselves, even though this is not always the best option for the needs of the business.

Regardless of individual managers' preferences, globalization and virtual teams have made centralization's application less effective in twenty-first-century business than it might have been previously. As a result, decentralization has become the most common contemporary business model.

Decentralization: Advantages and Disadvantages

We can readily see the advantages of decentralization, but here are some of the most essential ones:

- Decentralized decisions are usually reached more quickly.
- Decentralized decisions are usually more cost-effective.

- Decentralization results in fewer "detours," as it limits the amount of incorrect decisions resulting from loss of (or inadequate) information.
- Decentralization rejects authority based on status and emphasizes small, straightforward goals.
- Decentralization relieves management of detailed (expert) decisions, enabling more time for true management decisions.
- Decentralization results in employee empowerment, which stimulates greater commitment, increased enthusiasm, and more willingness to take on risk and responsibility.
- Decentralization of decision making is an excellent method for challenging and developing employees, as such a business model requires that they learn to make decisions on their own.

Its numerous and important advantages notwithstanding, decentralization can have certain disadvantages. For example, communication, coordination, and controls all become more difficult. For this reason, management should always combine decentralized decision making with a stronger centralization of controls and support. Such services as electronic data processing, market research, advertising, personnel recruitment, training, IT, etc., must be centralized and expanded constantly. Together with corporate guidelines and framework, they serve as the foundation for decentralized decision making. In other words, without an increase in centralized support, decentralized decision making is not very useful, at least not within a financially justifiable scope.

Decentralization certainly has fewer disadvantages than advantages, so it is better for most companies to opt for it. In addition, systems and operational processes (coordination system, communication system, and so on) all will help management overcome the disadvantages and maximize the effectiveness of a decentralized decision-making system. By and large, decentralization is preferable to centralization.

Based on these considerations, we can conclude that management should emphasize decentralization, particularly in difficult situations (e.g., times of crisis), as this is the time to maximize the advantages of decentralization. In corporate practice, however, the opposite is often the case: If everything is going smoothly (e.g., in boom conditions), management implements decentralization. But as soon as problems arise (e.g., during a downturn of the economy or when the company faces major problems), management centralizes procedures, resulting in all the known disadvantages with respect to performance. In order to avoid these negative outcomes, we must embrace the positive aspects of decentralization, which are the key contributing factors to its increased popularity. That said, it is critical to understand that optimal decentralization depends upon appropriate and effective *delegating*, as mentioned previously.

In order for delegating to work successfully, managers must initiate agreed-upon goals with employees (following requisite development), monitor performance continually, communicate clearly and consistently, and warn employees repeatedly in the event of subpar performance, such as delay in fulfilling the tasks in question. If the employees do not achieve the set goals, it will reflect poorly on both the employee and the manager, which is why managers hesitate to delegate! The solution is not to avoid delegating; the solution is to empower department managers to be responsible for all hiring, evaluating, and corrective action, seeking input from HR and/or upper management when needed. No manager will be willing to delegate if unable to handle with full authority the problems that will inevitably arise, including lackluster employee performance.

Now that we see how successful organizational structure hinges on effective use of management triangles and consistent delegating through decentralization (or centralization, if that is the company's preference), let's explore how these principles impact day-to-day operations.

Organizational Day-to-Day Operations

Whether decentralized or centralized, an organizational structure is the sum of the responsibilities for results of business units, based on the management triangle(s). Conversely, if an organizational chart cannot be represented by a management triangle, (avoidable) conflict sources are included in the organizational chart, which can have a permanent negative impact on effectiveness. Each employee should have a unique position with precisely described responsibilities and should be responsible for two or more positions only in exceptional cases (e.g., as a temporary solution, until a newly created position is filled).

Organizational structures have changed throughout the centuries. Historically, they began with the traditional staff/line organization still used in the military. Over time, other types of structures have emerged, notably divisional and matrix organizations. In today's business world, team organizations have become increasingly popular, as innovative onsite workplaces and virtual workplaces dominate the landscape.

There is no ideal organizational structure. Each has advantages and disadvantages. It is particularly counterproductive to introduce an organizational structure from the outside, just because it works well in another company or happens to be de rigueur. Many healthy corporate structures have been destroyed in this manner, much to the detriment of the companies in question.

Structuring Elements

The easiest and probably oldest principle for organizational structuring is the assignment of similar tasks to a majority of employees. This system is still found today where comparable positions are grouped into organizational units (e.g., salespersons, mailpersons, data-entry clerks, machinists, etc.).

Another classic structure, segmentation based on function (e.g., sales, marketing, production, procurement, accounting, IT, materials management, HR, manufacturing, etc.), is still common today, although it often no longer lives up to demands. A regional segmentation (branch offices in specific geographic locations) is another simple organizational structure. Contemporary organizational structures are based on product areas or markets; constructed with the intention of giving employees greater freedom and better identification opportunities, such structures are known as *profit centers*. Most companies today have a mixed structure based on function, markets, and regions. Let's further explore some of these structures in order to determine how to use each one with optimal effectiveness.

Departments

A *department* is an organization unit that carries out specific tasks and activities based on the knowledge of its experts. Most companies today still have departments as part of their organizational structure. Generally, a manager is responsible for each department, which includes expert staff. This is the case in centralized departments as well. Some companies still have (expert) support staff as part of the department, but this has been rarer over the past several years, especially because computerization has made secretaries and administrative assistants less necessary for lower-level managers and their teams.

For the most part, departments are components of larger groups called *functions*. (Some companies may call these divisions, or draw distinctions between functions and divisions. For clarity's sake we will limit our discussion of this level of organizational structure to functions.)

Advantages of the Departmental Organizational Structure

- good overview of individual departments; thus, good possibilities for controls of those departments
- uniformity of all departmentally bundled results

Disadvantages of the Departmental Organizational Structure

- frequently poor interdepartmental communication and interaction
- difficulty of horizontal coordination
- ability to create a rigid view of the company, as well as departmental egocentrism ("department-centric" view)

Functions

A *function* is an overarching area within a company, based upon the type of task or activity. As described above, multiple departments usually comprise each function. For our purposes, we can also think of a function as a group of interrelated departments.

For example, consider a corporation's finance function. Its component departments would likely include pricing, cost controls, measurements, general accounting, accounts receivable, accounts payable, and so on. An EVP, SVP, vice president, or group executive (depending on company nomenclature) would probably oversee the function, with directors reporting to him or her, and managers and employees all as respective direct reports right down the line according to the company's specific hierarchy.

In an ideal situation, such a structure promotes a clear chain of command and line of decision-making authority, with solid opportunities to use delegating, coordination, and controls all to maximum effect. In a less-than-ideal situation, of course, the opposite outcome occurs. Twenty-first-century changes—hyperconnectivity via the Internet, telecommuting, virtual teams, etc.—have created challenges for the functional organization structure. Nevertheless, it still has value.

Any organization in which management establishes responsibilities based upon the type of task or activity has a functional organizational structure.

FUNCTIONAL ORGANIZATIONAL STRUCTURE

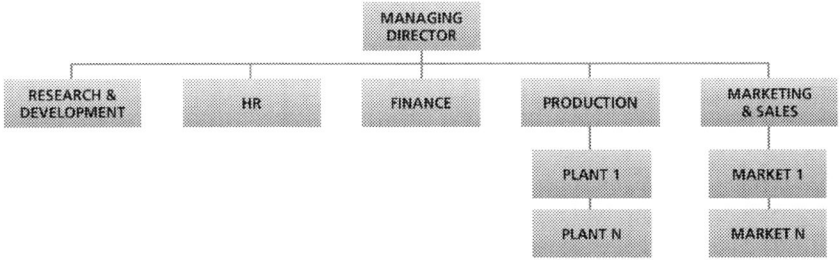

Figure 3-4: Functional Organizational Structure

Advantages of the Functional Organizational Structure

- good overview of individual functions; thus, good possibilities for controls of functions (e.g., for sales, manufacturing, HR, finance, accounting, IT, etc.)
- uniformity of all functionally bundled results (e.g., sales results, manufacturing results, and so on)

Disadvantages of the Functional Organizational Structure

- lack of oversight in the case of different products and markets
- length and difficulty of communication paths
    - difficulty of horizontal coordination
    - difficulty of identifying with a specific product or market (e.g., in a company with sixteen product lines, the sales department sells sixteen product lines, manufacturing produces sixteen product lines, R&D develops sixteen product lines, etc.; weak points are difficult to identify and correct)

(Note that the twenty-first-century challenges arising from globalization and virtual teams further augment the disadvantages inherent in functional organizational structures.)

Functional Staff

Although companies need staffs—including the central support staffs required by decentralization (HR, IT, accounting, administration, planning, etc.)—we must take care not to confuse staffs with the primarily outdated staff/line organization. A *staff* is essentially the same as a department. A staff/line organization is altogether different.

In the staff/line organizational structure, the decision-preparing entities (staff departments) are separated from the decision-making positions (lines). This is more the traditional model of the past, used extensively through the twentieth century in the vast majority of large corporations (and even smaller organizations).

In many cases, the functional organization has morphed into a hybrid or completely evolved into a staff/line organization. One reason for this is the desire to separate the decision-making authority from the decision-preparing positions within the company. In some cases this has led to curious organizational charts in which company managers no longer have clear supervisory oversight because of all the staff positions.

Consequently, many assume the traditional staff/line organization has no future. Because of the current trend toward broader and flatter organizational structures, the once-clear difference between staff and line has become fuzzy. Staff departments have become central service departments (IT, HR, market research, etc.), which no longer simply prepare decisions but have their own areas of decision making. (This must be so because of the ever-increasing division of labor in the twenty-first-century environment of hypertechnology.) This development includes even typical staff departments, such as assistants, secretaries, coordinators, etc. (Some companies attach support staff to expert departments and/or functions; others make them central service departments.)

When accurately defined and appropriately put into practice, the management concept eliminates the difference between staff and line. In fact, this is the whole premise of the triangle principle!

Advantages of a Staff/Line Organization

- Again, though used extensively for years, there are no advantages worth mentioning for our purpose. The twenty-first century has simply outgrown this model.

Disadvantages of the Staff/Line Organization

- In company practice, there is often disrespect toward staff employees who have the reputation of "only preparing" decisions and not making them.
- Staff departments tend to assume more decision-making authority than they are entitled to exhibit, so they often act as extensions of corporate management within companies.

Clearly, the traditional staff/line organization has no place in the twenty-first-century business world. However, a management concept that does work quite effectively in today's environment arose from the staff/line concept—or, perhaps, from an amalgam of function/staff/line. We call it the *team*.

Teams

Teams should require little, if any, explanation. For our purposes, *teams* are like departments, but their orientation is around achieving set goals, rather than on completing tasks or engaging in activities. To put this another way, teams center on motivation, whereas departments center on productivity. Teams primarily developed in large twentieth-century corporations that fostered the idea of "company as family," where the company valued employee loyalty, and employees, in turn, offered that loyalty without hesitation. Today's teams work, in part, because they offer employees something they want over and above a paycheck: working from home, tailoring hours to meet child-care needs, and so on.

Another reason why teams work effectively in today's business world is the changed "officescape," which now embraces *virtual teams* (discussed later in this chapter). That is, some employees work onsite, others work in satellite offices elsewhere in the country or anywhere in the world, and still others telecommute from home offices. Because of the motivating aspect of being part of a team, these disparate work options unite coworkers and go a long way toward minimizing or eliminating the friction and resentment that such alternative arrangements typically engendered in years past.

Advantages of the Team Organizational Structure

- positive identification with the team's objective (mission)
- strong collaboration (teamwork)
- high degree of enthusiasm, innovation, motivation, and initiative
- increased flexibility and resiliency among employees (team members)

Disadvantages of the Team Organizational Structure

- Lack of effective use of management tools can lead to poor results (team members who are not suited to working without strong supervision will flounder in this model).
- Weak managers can easily lose control of a team.

Project Organizations

Closely allied with the team is the *project organization*. The biggest difference between them is that team organizations can be of lasting duration, whereas project organizations end when the project is complete.

Project organizations are self-explanatory: they carry out a special task (project), and management dissolves them when the project is finished. (Today's project organizations operate similarly to the task forces of large corporations during the twentieth century.)

Project organization entails the multifunction coordination of planning, governance, and decision-making processes in the event of challenges of a wide scope. Although most similar to the team, the key difference between project organization and other organizational structures is the temporal nature of the component projects.

Frequent Sources of Errors and Problems in Project Organizations

- There is a lack of coordination among the various parties participating in a project, resulting in time and cost disadvantages.
- There are unrealistic schedules.
- The project manager lacks decision-making authority toward the persons participating in the project; the participants do not see their priorities in the project, but in other tasks, and therefore do not show sufficient commitment to the project.
- During the duration of the project, new requests are included, jeopardizing the original project goals.

Information and decision-making are subject to change, which can jeopardize the desired result of the project. In order to avoid the above risks, observe the following organizational principles:

- Project manager must have clearly formulated responsibility for results.
- Project manager must have clearly formulated decision-making authority.
- Project participants must agree upon clearly formulated project goals.
- Project participants must identify with the project through intensive preparation; the time and employees required for the project must be planned by participants, and must be taken into consideration in their goals and objectives.

Matrix Organizations

The *matrix organization* (see figure 3-2, as well as the true-to-life business scenario at the beginning of this chapter) is one in which an objective-related organizational structure like a network overlays the foundational functional organizational structure; that is, vertical administrative functions are connected to horizontal tasks, areas, processes, and/or projects. In large, complex companies, matrix organizations provide managerial oversight, as well as governance and controls (which we will discuss in chapter 4).

The matrix organization contains a reduced number of organizational levels, creating a flattened hierarchy. Within this structure, redundant functions and checks and balances are eliminated in favor of clear goals, objectives, accountabilities, and performance measurements. Advocates of the matrix organization share a common view of the benefits of working this way. This structure also lends itself to rich and rapid communication. The true-to-life business scenario at the beginning of this chapter illustrates the benefits of the matrix organization.

All that said, there is no ideal system or structure. The matrix organization is no exception, and it can lead to a difficult balance of power. Matrix structures are very well suited to developing new activities and effectively coordinating complicated processes with complex dependencies. They are not suitable for employees who need to have a good overview of their workplace, or who are highly dependent colleagues or supervisors. Matrix structures require considerable group-dynamic capabilities from employees, as well as a high degree of tolerance for ambiguous situations.

Advantages of the Matrix Organizational Structure

- enables better solutions because the right people and skill sets are involved from the beginning
- promotes integrated solutions through the use of cross-functional expertise
- encourages stronger communication between functions, departments, teams, and project teams (project organizations)
- reduces the amount of bureaucracy
- creates an adaptive structure of people and resources that can focus on the most immediate business needs
- develops deeper expertise in staff

Disadvantages of the Matrix Organizational Structure

- potential duplication of effort if communication is not clear and timely
- potential for slower client responsiveness because of multiple priorities
- less focused; there isn't one "right" way to approach tasks, problems, etc.
- responsibilities may not be well-defined
- difficulty in balancing the needs of multiple "bosses"
- conflicts over priorities

Profit Centers

A *profit center* is an autonomous organizational unit, often an organizational component in a larger company, which independently provides results within the scope of certain guidelines, and which is only responsible for a few basic results. In an extreme case, this could mean results for a profit margin, or profit to a previously determined extent. (*Business segment organization* is another term often used for a profit center.)

As a whole, every company is a profit center. Based on this, it seems tempting to also allow partial areas of a company to act as an independent company (company within a company, independent line of business, etc.). The goal is increased flexibility and better performance. This tendency toward independence may lead so far that a profit center, which previously marketed the products manufactured within its own company, can also purchase these products externally. This supposedly puts competitive pressure on the company's own manufacturing division, ensuring exploration of every opportunity to improve productivity.

Because there are many areas in a company which "only" create costs and do not yield profits, they are not profit centers in the true sense. Nevertheless, these areas can also be rendered independent, with the task of only producing certain core results. In these cases, the term *result center* is more appropriate. One condition must be met in all cases: only one manager can head a profit/result center. Needless to say, in corporate practice, this requirement is often disregarded.

Profit centers may be organized with different characteristics, such as markets, regions, etc.

Advantages of Profit Centers

- reward for entrepreneurial initiative
- quick adaptation to modified conditions with respect to market and technology
- good separation of responsibility for results and decision-making authority through decentralization
- short communication paths
- good opportunities for effective controls
- in general, better performance, higher productivity, and higher profits

Disadvantages of Profit Centers

- risk of drifting apart ("company within a company"), thereby creating greater need for coordination
- problems created by clients buying from more than one profit center

Optimal Organizational Structure

Again, there is no ideal organizational structure. Each company must be organized based on its individual needs. The crucial issue is whether or not a company is able to adapt to changing environments by changing its organizational structure. The inability to achieve such an adaptation has resulted in significant difficulties for companies, and in extreme cases, even in bankruptcy. Flexibility can only be achieved if all members of the organization identify with it and are willing to challenge their own position within the organizational chart. This is best achieved by including all affected parties in all questions concerning responsibilities, modifications of the structure, etc. (This often involves implementing change management, as described in chapter 2.)

Although there is no ideal organizational structure, there are guidelines for evaluating effectiveness. Better profit centers are generally the result of more-effective and more-flexible organizational structures. Flexibility is key to both effectiveness and profitability in the twenty-first-century business world.

A functional organization can also implement the profit-center idea by assuring a large degree of freedom for the individual positions and making them responsible for as few core results as possible. In this sense, the profit center best corresponds to the principles of effective corporate management stipulated by the management concept. Having studied various types of organizations, we can readily understand why organization is an easy-to-use tool that is nonetheless frequently misunderstood. Now let's turn our attention to another system that is essential to contemporary business: the *virtual team*.

Virtual Team

A virtual team refers to any group of employees using information technologies (IT) and other communications systems in order to collaborate from different workplaces. As mentioned earlier, such workplaces can be in different parts of a single large building, in different parts of the country, or in different countries; virtual team members may work onsite or in home offices. Clearly, virtual teams can create conflicts, complications, and challenges, but they offer many benefits. Taking all that into consideration, let's see how our examination of organizational structures relates to the twenty-first century.

Effective Organizational Structure in the World of Working Remotely

Ideally, managers should focus on management triangles, profit centers, flexibility, and effectiveness in organization (in concert with the other management tools, of course). However, we must always keep in mind that today's workplace is vastly different from yesterday's, and it changes constantly. Computerization, the Internet, and social media all play key roles in this, and whether employees are onsite, offsite, or at-home working via teleportation, virtual teams are the way of the world. In the foreseeable future, all this will likely continue and further intensify.

Although telecommuting is clearly entrenched in corporate culture, there are companies that are returning to the roots of onsite employment. The reason for this is that employees housed in the same space are generally more innovative, even though employees who work from home are usually more productive. Each organization needs to determine which is more important, innovation or productivity, before deciding upon a policy for this. In addition, management styles, strategic planning and goal setting, organizational structure, and communication all are major contributing factors to such a decision. The quality of management received always dictates the quality of employee results. Environment in and of itself does not foster or hinder productivity or innovation. Effective managers always remain mindful of this. Suffice it to say that telecommuting in the absence of effective organizational structure (as well as the other key tools) can create a ripple effect of negative outcomes. With virtual teams, as with every system, the buck stops with the manager—that's just the way it is.

Applying What You Have Learned

As the core statement opening this chapter emphasizes, organization is an easy-to-use tool, but often misunderstood. We managers must make sure to remember that, and our day-to day management must always include clear communication, clear line of authority, and clear decision making, as clarity in these areas is essential to effectiveness and success.

Here are some essential steps related to organization that we all need to implement:

1. Utilize the key management tool of organization, including effective management triangles and a clear system of decentralization or centralization (depending upon company needs).
2. Ensure clear line of authority and decision making, appropriately cascaded to all levels.
3. Establish effective systems and procedures for whichever type of organization the company uses (e.g., matrix, profit center, etc.), as well as the virtual teams that dominate the twenty-first-century business landscape.

By incorporating the above items 1 through 3 into our daily routine, we are well on the way to becoming effective managers. And that's "simply management"!

Now that we've thoroughly discussed organizational structure, let's turn to another key management tool: governance and controls, which we will explore in the next chapter.

4

GOVERNANCE AND CONTROLS

Controls refer to the past; governance refers to the future.

Definition of Governance and Controls

Governance is the alignment of general conditions used to achieve goals and to limit the scope of decision-making authority through appropriate cascading. *Controls* involve the effective monitoring, regulation, and direction of operations, budgets, performance, and so on. Another way to think of this is that governance refers to expected future behavior, while controls refer to measurements used to determine the extent of effective adherence to governance, or the deviation from it.

Furthermore, effective governance and controls depend upon effective strategic planning, goal setting, and organizational structure. Without planning, targets and goals cannot be set or determined. Without organizational structure, a clear chain of command and line of decision-making authority cannot be established. Of course, none of these can work optimally without clear communication. As seen in previous chapters, all these essential management tools and techniques must be used in concert, as they work synergistically.

The true-to-life business scenario that follows examines the use of governance and controls, showing how essential their effective use can be to company success. Let's see why this is so.

True-to-Life Business Scenario: Effective Governance and Controls Are Key to Company Success

INPO Corporation is a global manufacturer of high-tech global positioning systems. Given that they are a company that has grown via global acquisitions and has worked in a matrix organizational structure for more than ten years, INPO had almost no global information technology (IT) governance or controls in place. (Each of the acquired companies had their own IT resources and processes.) In order to support the growing demands of a global organization and ensure clarity and transparency of decision making, oversight, and even simple visibility into all functions within INPO, Shelia, the chief information officer (CIO), has taken on the task of building a global governance system (complete with supporting controls) for the organization's IT.

Governance is defined as *the action or manner of governing*. In order to create a global IT governance structure, Shelia will need to identify the governance leadership (or board), consider their interests, roles, and responsibilities, as well as clarify the behaviors (ethics, integrity, transparency, etc.) required of the leadership. In the end, Shelia's goal is to have a governance that establishes a standard approach to process and approvals that support organizational alignment and drive company values.

To start, Shelia established an IT governance board comprised of the CIO (Shelia), the global director of infrastructure, the global director of architecture, and the regional IT directors for each of the respective regions in Europe, Asia, North America, and South America. The board then drafted and approved the governance document, which included

- IT Governance Model Purpose
- IT Mission and Vision
- Guiding Principles
- Leadership Responsibilities
- IT Governance Scope
- Portfolio Management

- Project Approval or Scope/Direction Change
- IT Governance Meetings

Once the governance document was approved by the board, the global IT team had a clear understanding of the way forward.

But they didn't stop there. Shelia knew that for a governance model to be sustainable, it had to be thoroughly communicated across the organization. And the IT governance board had to model the governance every step of the way. One way to ensure sustainability of the model is via controls. Controls provide a clear, metric-based view of the past, in order to ensure that the governance is followed. They may be referred to as key performance indicators (KPIs), metrics, or even specific goals tied to performance. Each team at INPO accordingly identified controls that allowed them to keep a close eye on the status of the organization, as well as their alignment with overall business success.

Therefore, by building a global governance model for the organization, not only did Shelia (and the team) clarify their roles, responsibilities, and the organization's purpose/vision, they also provided a pathway for their entire company that will drive decisions, projects, and initiatives and that will build team continuity.

As the above true-to-life business scenario illustrates, appropriately cascaded governance and controls are essential to business success and managerial effectiveness in the global environment of the twenty-first century. In addition to the benefits they provide to global management, governance and controls ensure effectiveness among virtual teams as well.

Let's now turn our attention toward a deeper discussion of the purpose and importance of the key management tool of governance and controls.

Purpose and Importance of Governance and Controls

As we've already seen, governance and controls together comprise a two-pronged essential management tool. Governance addresses management's expectations for the future, while controls measure how effectively employees followed the established expectations. Both governance and controls depend upon clearly communicated goals and plans and a clearly established chain of command and line of decision-making authority. This entire system must be cascaded appropriately at every level.

Furthermore, every plan must include individual steps monitored by established controls that employees are aware of. That is, every employee must know what is controlled, when, and by whom. As seen in the true-to-life business scenario, management's role must be visible. In other words, the better the plan, the more precise the governance and controls can be. The more precise the governance and controls are, the more effectively management can carry them out. In terms of the bottom line, there is no way to compare the target to the actual unless there is a predetermined target in the first place.

Inadequate or improper planning renders controls meaningless: if you don't know where you want to go, it doesn't matter where you are.

All that said, in management, governance is more important than controls. (Considering the overall time allocation to governance and controls, 80 percent of time should be spent on the former, 20 percent on the latter.) The future is likely to be different from the past, so the analysis of the past only offers limited conclusions. Remember, governance refers to the future, controls to the past. As managers, we should focus more on influencing the future than on analyzing past mistakes and searching for their causes, despite the commonly pursued quest to do so. The ideal system is to establish effective governance and controls and then utilize the controls merely to assess the governance in order to determine if adjustments are necessary. If they are, management should take the steps required to implement them; if they are not, further analysis of the past is simply unnecessary and serves no purpose.

Governance Methods and Measurements

Governance Framework

In order to be able to offer employees complete freedom in performing their tasks and to hold them responsible for achieving measurable results, it is necessary to first establish a governance framework, which includes an unambiguous, easy-to-follow system and a process that management clearly explains and communicates to all employees, preferably in conjunction with a written document. Such a document (which may include graphics as enhancing elements, if necessary) should be designed to provide further reinforcement for employees; this is another way to encourage employee empowerment, as unambiguous systems allow for confident self-monitoring and self-correcting. In short, this framework should empower employees, not restrict or impede them. Therefore, within the framework, employees have the freedom and authority to determine the daily work flow in their respective areas of responsibility.

It is therefore extremely important for every employee to actively participate in establishing his or her own framework. The superior only intervenes to advise and assist, and to correct if the employee deviates from the established governance system (framework or process). The amount of decision-making authority cascaded to specific levels within the organization should determine the extent of individual employee empowerment. Once employees receive individual decision-making authority, they can then make decisions freely within that system.

GOVERNANCE PROCESS

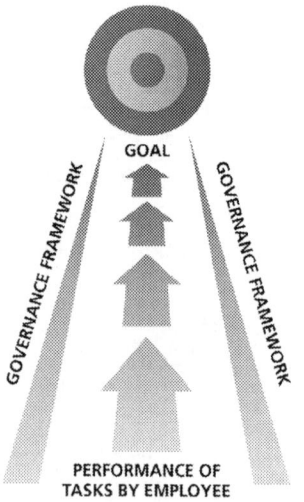

Figure 4-1: Governance Process

Principles of Governance

Remember, governance is a system that makes employees aware of management's expectations. Before performing any task, all employees must know

- what results management expects,
- what decision-making authority they (employees) have,
- what help they (employees) may expect, and
- what recognition they (employees) will receive.

After finishing any task, employees should not have to ask, "Did I do this right?" The established governance should let them know the answer ahead of executing the task. Governance must always be unambiguous. All employees must be able to understand and easily follow every governance system.

Ideally, management should clearly express the desired results for any tasks or responsibilities *before* employees undertake those tasks or responsibilities. Again, this means that the governance framework should be clear and unambiguous, so that employees have no doubt as to whether they have accomplished the desired results. This should be self-evident, but its importance cannot be overemphasized.

The more a system of governance provides employees with the possibility of monitoring and correcting their own performance and results, the better that system is.

Remember, of the time allocated to governance and controls, 80 percent should go to governance, and 20 percent should go to controls. That means managers should spend a significant amount of time discussing all the parameters, challenges, issues, and potential problems *before* employees undertake their respective tasks. This is effective governance. Managers who approach governance in this manner need astonishingly little time for controls.

In addition, by empowering employees, management engages them in the process. Such employees feel invested, readily ensuring their buy-in and cooperation. Effective results centers use governance and controls to optimal effect, and everyone concerned benefits—it becomes a perennial win-win system for employees, management, and the company as a whole.

Management by Exception

A new governance concept, *management by exception,* has established itself in recent years, offering significant advantages. It is a system of governance in which only deviations from the norm (framework or process) are to be reported to the manager, ensuring that management attention is only given when necessary. This greatly simplifies the management process, making it transparent for all participants, and allowing each manager to focus only on the problems that require the most attention. Simply put, the manager no longer needs to deal with day-to-day issues that are better left to employees to handle.

Management by exception notifies managers when they must get involved, and also gauges how long such involvement will likely be. This concept hinges on effective delegating, a clear line of decision-making authority, open and direct communication, and well-established, comprehensive governance and controls. Management involvement only happens if extreme breaches of the governance system (framework or process) have occurred.

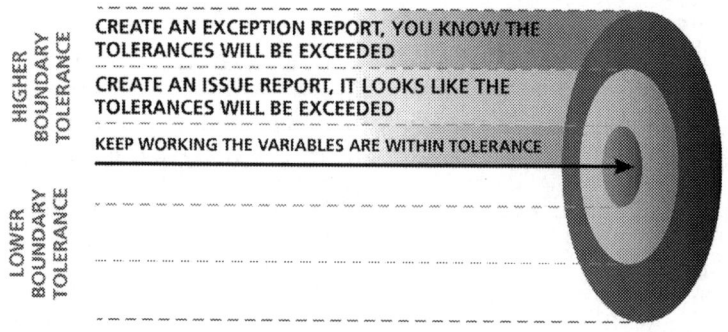

HOW TO WORK WITH TOLERANCE LEVELS

HIGHER BOUNDARY TOLERANCE

CREATE AN EXCEPTION REPORT, YOU KNOW THE TOLERANCES WILL BE EXCEEDED

CREATE AN ISSUE REPORT, IT LOOKS LIKE THE TOLERANCES WILL BE EXCEEDED

KEEP WORKING THE VARIABLES ARE WITHIN TOLERANCE

LOWER BOUNDARY TOLERANCE

Figure 4-2: Management by Exception

EXAMPLES OF BREACHES OF THE GOVERNANCE SYSTEM
COSTS EXCEEDED BY $X OR X%
TIME EXCEEDED BY X NUMBER OF UNITS (DAYS, WEEKS, MONTHS, ETC.)
DEFECTIVE GOODS RATE OF X NUMBER OF UNITS OR X% PER TIME UNIT
X NUMBER OR X% OF CUSTOMER COMPLAINTS/RETURNS PER TIME UNIT

Example of Areas Where Management by Exception Is Effective

HUMAN RESOURCES (HR)
PERSONNEL COSTS
OVERTIME
PRODUCTION/MANUFACTURING
DEFECTIVE PRODUCTS
MATERIAL COSTS
MATERIAL USAGE
MACHINE UTILIZATION
UNITS PRODUCED
SALES
NEW CUSTOMERS
CUSTOMER COMPLAINTS
FLUCTUATION
CLOSING QUOTA
MISCELLANEOUS
TRAVEL EXPENSES
ADVERTISING EXPENSES
PROJECT MANAGEMENT

Advantages of Management by Exception

- It facilitates quick reaction and response to deviations.
- Managers only focus on exceptions and extenuating circumstances, which relieves them of a considerable amount of time and effort spent "putting out fires" on a day-to-day basis.
- Employees have the opportunity to be the first to recognize deviations and develop their own self-correcting process. This empowers them to take initiative, evaluate their own work, and resolve problems.
- It saves time and resources.
- It's more cost-effective.
- It simplifies the decision-making process.
- It facilitates objective evaluation of employees by emphasizing assessment of results.

Governance Results

Effective controls assess the results of governance. Remember, the purpose of controls is to review the extent to which employees followed the governance system—and how successful that system was. The administration of those results, as well as the assessment of their effectiveness and value (comparison of target and actual), is a task a manager cannot delegate.

Only managers can administer and assess the results of governance by means of controls.

Assessing the results of governance, again, is the use of controls: the evaluation of the extent to which an employee has achieved, or failed to achieve, a certain result. Such controls must rely on established measurements that should be consistent throughout the company and cascaded appropriately to all levels.

When governance is effective, it should be necessary to only spend a minimal amount of time on controls. Changes to the governance system should only occur if the controls assessment determines either or both of the following:

1. Implementing a different procedure could have achieved an improved result.
2. There are gaps in the development of the employee.

Managers should not assess performance (initiate controls) while an employee is still completing a task. They should always wait until results are available, as this will provide for appropriate measurement of both the governance system and employee performance. However, in extreme situations where a manager observes unsatisfactory performance of an in-process task (even in instances of management-by-exception governance systems), he or she should either change existing elements of governance or establish new ones together with the employee. This allows the controls tool to become a development tool, benefiting the employee. If the employee's performance improves, the manager can then determine whether the governance system requires any adjustment, and can seek input from colleagues as appropriate. (Input from colleagues prior to acting is crucial to effective governance, as we saw with the building of the IT team in the true-to-life business scenario at the beginning of this chapter.)

Requirements of an Effective Governance System

An effective governance system must be:

- clearly and unambiguously presented, explained, and communicated to all employees
- complete with a framework and process that are easy to understand and easy to follow
- cascaded appropriately throughout all levels of the company
- accompanied by written documents that employees can refer to for reinforcement
- focused on achieving mutually agreed-upon results
- established together with the employee (discussed, not dictated)

- created to empower employees with decision-making authority and freedom within that framework
- designed for precise measurability (time, quantity, quality, etc.) to work synergistically with accompanying controls (that assess the governance)
- suitable as an employee-development instrument

Controls Methods and Measurements

Principles of Controls

The controls process consists of addressing the items listed in the following table:

PRINCIPLES OF CONTROLS

TARGET PERFORMANCE	WHAT DID WE WANT TO ACHIEVE?
ACTUAL PERFORMANCE	WHAT DID WE ACTUALLY ACHIEVE?
DEVIATION	WHICH POSITIVE OR NEGATIVE DIFFERENCE EXISTS BETWEEN TARGET AND ACTUAL FIGURES? WHAT ARE THE REASONS FOR THIS DEVIATION?
CORRECTIVE MEASURES	WHAT ARE WE GOING TO DO NOW, IN ORDER TO CONTINUE THE POSITIVE DEVELOPMENT OR AVOID ANY NEGATIVE DEVELOPMENTS IN THE FUTURE?

Note that corrective measures close the controlling cycle because they provide measures for the future.

CONTROLS PROCESS

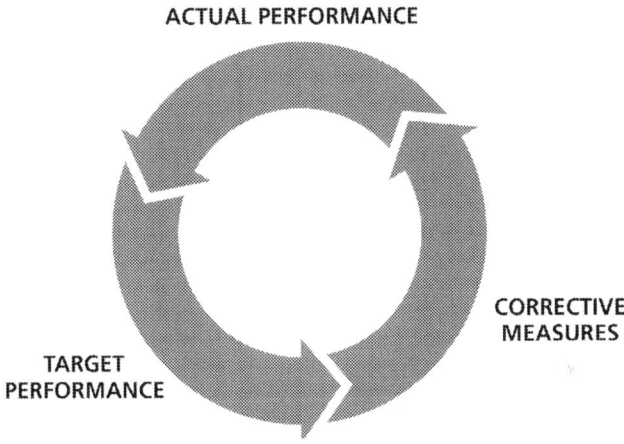

Figure 4-3: Controls Process

Strong monitoring of employees (often referred to as "micromanaging") is usually not effective. In the contemporary environment of globalization and virtual teams, it is no longer possible to "look over everyone's shoulder" as a way to prevent something from going wrong. Fortunately, it is no longer necessary to do so. When employees know and understand the conditions of the governance system (framework and process), managers seldom have to deal with employees' individual decisions. In addition, in order to promote employee development, superiors should not involve themselves in these day-to-day decisions once employees have received decision-making authority. (This applies to management by exception, as well as any effective governance system [framework and process].) If employees accept that empowerment, they must also accept the accountability and responsibility it entails. Allow them to step up and do so.

There is another extremely simple way of looking at this: managers should use controls to monitor results, not employees.

Many superiors inaccurately believe that their main duty is to point out employees' mistakes, in an effort to correct them (and avoid mistakes in the future). This is ineffective. Again, managers more effectively spend their time and resources by establishing clear and useful systems of governance. Therefore, they should provide employees with all the information they need to monitor their own performance, correcting as necessary, and they should provide this in a timely manner—ahead of employees' starting the task, whenever possible. This is key to effective controls (and the governance they evaluate), as well as to effective employee development (which we will discuss in the next chapter). Managers who create controls systems that enable them to see employee mistakes before the employees themselves become aware of them are not acting as managers. It is quite counterproductive that many controls systems are structured and tailored toward the superior, not the employee. (Again, this impedes the effectiveness of not only governance and controls, but employee development as well.)

In short, the best controls system is the one that employees control themselves. This empowers employees, increases their performance, enhances their development, and allows management to allocate 20 percent of governance-and-controls time to controls, as is optimal.

Requirements of an Effective Controls System

An effective controls system must

- be tailored toward completion of the task;
- focus on assessing the results, not the person (employee);
- empower employees with decision-making authority and freedom within the established framework;
- be designed for precise measurability (time, quantity, quality, etc.);
- coordinate in collaboration with the affected employee (determined together, not dictated);
- focus on avoiding mistakes in the future (this works synergistically with governance; the past cannot be changed or corrected, so a costly analysis of committed errors does not make very much sense);
- be geared toward a meaningful comparison of target and actual values;
- be suitable as an employee-development instrument; and
- be established and communicated in written form, if possible.

Applying What You Have Learned

As the core statement opening this chapter emphasizes, controls refer to the past, governance to the future. It is always essential for managers to focus more on the future (governance) than the past (controls), so governance and controls should receive an 80/20 allocation of time, respectively. Managers who practice this are generally more effective, as their employees feel empowered, engaged, and valued. We must remember too that governance and controls hinge on effectively established strategic planning and goal setting—and all of these depend upon clear communication appropriately cascaded throughout all levels.

Here are some essential steps related to governance and controls that we all need to implement:

1. Utilize the key management tool of governance and controls, including future-oriented focus and employee empowerment and self-monitoring.
2. Ensure clear and unambiguous decision-making authority, appropriately cascaded to all levels.
3. Establish an effective governance system (framework and process), which will automatically lead to a minimal amount of time and effort spent on controls; this is essential for success in the atmosphere of globalization and virtual teams that dominate the twenty-first-century business landscape.

By incorporating the above items 1 through 3 into our daily routine, we are well on the way to becoming effective managers. And that's "simply management"!

Now that we've thoroughly discussed governance and controls, let's turn to another key management tool: employee development and advancement, which we will explore in the next chapter.

5

EMPLOYEE DEVELOPMENT
AND ADVANCEMENT

A manager's skill is best measured by increased employee performance.

Definition of Employee Development and Advancement

Employee development refers to the enhancement of the skills, knowledge, and experiences of employees, with the purpose and intention of improving their performance. Employee development systems design and implement methods and measures that will help employees increase overall performance by achieving better results and taking on more responsibilities. (Employee development focuses strictly on performance at work. It is career-oriented and should never be confused with personal development/growth.)

Employee advancement refers to management's preparing employees to take on additional responsibilities, beyond those encouraged during the development phase. In fact, advancement is the next natural step following development. However, we must make a clear distinction: advancement is not promotion. Promotions should follow requisite employee development and advancement and should reflect instances where specific employees have fulfilled all previous responsibilities exceptionally well. In other words, promotions are management's way of acknowledging outstanding performance and indicating that these employees have proved themselves capable of taking on a role with greater responsibility. (As opposed to greater responsibilities within their original roles, which would be advancement.)

Employee development and advancement must be used in concert with the other essential management tools and techniques in order to be maximally effective. Organizational structure, governance and controls, and communication all are key to achieving effectiveness in employee development and advancement. Remember, every manager's skill is best measured by increased improvement in employee performance.

The true-to-life business scenario that follows illustrates effective and ineffective methods of employee development and advancement. Let's examine the difference between the two methods in order to create the most effective methods possible for actual use in the workplace.

True-to-Life Business Scenario: Effective and Ineffective Methods of Employee Development

Effective Method of Employee Development

Sam has been with SMART Industries for approximately two years. Early on, Sam's manager, Sarah, recognized him as an employee with high potential. Within his first two years with the organization, Sam was promoted once and had very strong performance evaluations.

The first thing that Sarah did regarding Sam's development was to ask him to share his short- and long-term goals. Sarah then shared Sam's goals with HR, her colleagues, and senior executives who had worked with Sam. Sarah considered the feedback received, and then she reviewed with Sam several career paths that he could pursue. Sam expressed which career path most interested him. Sarah and Sam then identified the key competencies and key experiences for the next targeted position. They both reviewed these experiences and competencies in order to determine what would be required for Sam to move from his current position to the targeted position within three to five years and also within five to ten years.

Next, Sarah and Sam created a development plan. They met on a regular basis to review progress. Sam's career development was a collaborative effort as Sarah and Sam built a development plan comprised of experiences and training. Sarah also recommended that Sam enroll in the company's mentoring program. Sam's mentor provided career guidance, as well as tips on how to influence others and how to work with senior leaders. Sam's mentor was someone who had followed a career path similar to Sam's. An extra bonus was that the mentor also currently held one of the positions that Sam aspired to obtain. The manager and mentor served different roles: The manager's role was to manage Sam's performance and employee development. The mentor's role was to coach Sam's progress.

Because Sam and Sarah were disciplined in executing the development plan—and because they each were accountable for their individual role and responsibility in making it happen—Sam was fast-tracked to his promotion to the targeted position within SMART Industries.

This is an instance of effective employee development. Sarah clearly recognizes that her managerial skill is measured through Sam's increased performance.

Ineffective Method of Employee Development

Jack has been with Washout Machine Company for approximately five years. Jack accepted a lateral move within Washout (with the understanding and coaching from functional leadership) to better position himself to learn more about the business and advance his career. He moved to a less-desirable location in order to learn and grow and as a result was assigned a different manager.

Jack expressed to his new manager that he wanted to broaden his career path and prepare himself to grow within the company. Unfortunately, Jack's new manager did not value or understand employee development. Jack continued to express to his manager his desire to map out a path for his future. However, the manager was more focused on Jack's performing his current job responsibilities and gave no attention to Jack's career development.

Because of all this, Jack did not have the opportunity for someone (manager or mentor) to guide and help him map out a career path. Consequently, Jack felt frustrated, abandoned, and misled. Within a year, Jack left the Washout Machine Company.

This is an instance of ineffective employee development. Jack's manager has no awareness that his own skill and effectiveness are measured by means of his employee's increased performance. In addition, with no development offered, Jack cannot maximize his full potential as an employee.

As the above true-to-life business scenario's two examples clearly show, SMART Industries uses effective employee development methods, whereas Washout Machine Company does not. Effective employee development entails managers' involvement in developing employees through performance evaluations and the development tool, as well as engaging mentors to coach employees' progress. (Note that the mentor is never the employee's manager.) Remember that the best measurement of any manager's skill is increased employee performance.

Employee Development Methods and Measurements

Effective managers accord equal importance to tasks, goals, employees, and their own managerial roles and responsibilities. This is managerial responsibility and competence in a nutshell. Competent and effective managers also commit to maintaining productivity, personal satisfaction, and team satisfaction. All this factors into effective employee development, using the essential methods and measurements at a manager's disposal.

Essential Development Methods

Employee development involves conveying knowledge and empowering decision making based on experience and sound judgment. An employee attains knowledge through training, education, and the transfer of knowledge from others. Sound judgment can only be learned through experience, but good decision making hinges on it. Most managers have been making decisions for so long that they tend to forget that the only way to learn how to make effective decisions is to make them—even if it means making mistakes. Mistakes are part of the learning process. This is a crucial aspect of employee development, and yet, it is the one that most managers resist. Many employees resist it too, simply because management perpetuates the fear of mistake-induced problems. Every effective decision maker has made mistakes, and learned from them. Resisting the process will not benefit employees, managers, or the company.

Practicing effective employee development is a requisite management responsibility. Employee development refers strictly to the individual's career, not to personal growth. As such, it occurs in the workplace, and the direct superior performs all aspects of it. If an employee has a mentor, that person should not be his or her manager. (The true-to-life business scenario at the beginning of this chapter illustrates an example of effective employee development and mentorship, as well as an example of ineffective development, which also reflects a lack of mentorship.)

We will discuss the challenges of decision making vis-à-vis employee development later on in this chapter (see Employee Development Obstacles). For now, let's focus on the transfer of knowledge, which is also essential to managerial effectiveness and success. In the course of employee development, the transfer of knowledge is usually a smooth process. Most employees are eager to learn and increase their performance.

But this is just the first step. Increased knowledge and the resultant increased performance (or lack of either) should be a clear indicator of employee aptitude (or inaptitude) for the job. In other words, employee development should assist managers with the task of getting as close as possible to the ideal state of having "the right person in the right job." This ideal state applies to every position within the company. Of course, no employee is perfect, and no company is perfect. In practical terms, every employee may not fulfill 100 percent of his or her job responsibilities. In many cases, 100 percent fulfillment of all responsibilities is impossible to accomplish. This is the case because of both the company's requirements and the constantly changing workforce. Nevertheless, it is every manager's responsibility to strive for this ideal state, and the most effective way to do so is through employee development. In essence, the manager "develops the employee into his or her area of responsibility." In so doing, the superior must try to increase each employee's knowledge and skills, eliminating any existing gaps or inadequacies. In certain circumstances, the manager must also reduce any undesired levels of performance (whether overperformance or underperformance in an area), if it is hindering the employee's overall performance.

Effective managers remain aware of the foregoing, and they also recognize that the "ideal" employee is rarely a new recruit from the outside (i.e., a new hire); more often than not, he or she has increased performance as a result of development within the company (both by the manager and mentors, where appropriate). When utilized in this manner, we can readily see the importance of employee development. The development of employees is a manager's most important task. Recall the original concept of management described in chapter 1: "causing employees to achieve goals" and "focusing on managerial tasks and delegating expert responsibilities." Simply put, management is not the execution of tasks, but the development of employees so that they can better achieve company goals.

Remember, a manager's skill is best measured by increased employee performance. The better the employees, the better their superior—and the better the entire company.

Essential Development Measurements

Employee development and advancement require effective measurements, as well as effective methods. In fact, the measurements assess the methods. Both ensure that management evaluates employee results, not characteristics or personality traits. To put this another way, development should not and cannot center on mere advice, such as "Improve your sociability" or "Try to limit your tendency to miss deadlines"; such comments, no matter how well-intentioned they might be, are not useful because they are subjective. In order for development to be effective and of maximal usefulness, it must be objective, concrete, and measurable. This enables both managers and employees to focus on results in a clear manner that is devoid of emotion. In addition, managers must design concrete development measures together with each employee, so that all measurements are mutually agreed upon. This fosters empowerment and buy-in because it identifies any gaps in experience and/or knowledge, allowing employees to step up and offer improved ways of performing tasks (with management agreement and approval). Used in this manner, development measurements empower employees while simultaneously enabling managers to enhance their own value through increased employee performance—a key managerial goal, as emphasized in this chapter's opening core statement.

Development Measurement Criteria

Development measurements refer to the completion of certain tasks, which are necessary to achieve goals, and which describe the satisfactory completion of those tasks. Again, to maximize effectiveness, managers must ensure that these measurements are mutually agreed upon, so that each employee clearly understands the paths required to achieve all goals, including all governance, controls, and any other pertinent systems, processes, strategies, etc. Providing any necessary clarification, whether because of complicated circumstances or lack of employee understanding, is a key management responsibility. Development cannot occur in the midst of confusion, and development gaps must be closed in order for employees to succeed. Lack of employee success will likely be viewed as the result of ineffective management.

The following table provides the necessary measurement criteria for effective employee development.

MEASUREMENT CRITERIA

QUALITY	WHAT DO WE EXPECT OF THE RESULTS?
QUANTITY	HOW MANY RESULTS DO WE EXPECT?
TIME	WHAT TURNAROUND DO WE EXPECT?
MONEY	WHAT DO WE EXPECT THE RESULTS TO COST?

Based on the above and similar criteria, a satisfactory execution of responsibilities becomes measurable. Here, both the superior and employee have the opportunity to define priorities and agree on the path that will lead to achievement of one goal or multiple goals. By using consistent measurements, managers can better gauge results in instances where multiple employees all have the same responsibilities for achieving results, even if their development measures are not identical (which they really cannot be, as different individuals can never have the exact same performance capabilities).

Furthermore, as we've seen in our discussions throughout this book, globalization and virtual teams have dramatically changed the corporate landscape. Employee development and advancement figure prominently in this, as opportunities abound, and the aspiration to remain employed in the same company for years on end is, as the saying goes, "So twentieth century." Remote workplaces—whether offsite, at-home, or in another country—limit managers' ability to observe employees firsthand on a continual basis. This makes effective measurements that much more critical, and managers must remain mindful of the importance of employee-assessment instruments.

All this brings us to the next crucial employee development measure: the performance evaluation.

Performance Evaluations

The current practice of employee evaluation is not satisfactory in many companies. Employees are usually either evaluated irregularly and spontaneously without a formal method, or at regular intervals on the basis of an evaluation system that has been introduced as mandatory for the company. Let's take a brief look at these less-than-ideal methods, after which we will explore more-effective ways to utilize the evaluation method.

Mandatory Evaluation Systems

In most companies, performance-evaluation systems are based on personality and character traits. Therefore, in order to competently perform and assess such evaluations, superiors would have to be trained in psychology. These measurement systems very rarely pose the question that is key to assessing employee performance: To what degree has the employee achieved the mutually agreed-upon goals and objectives? Employees work in companies in order to achieve certain results; thus, evaluations of their performance must be results-oriented in order to be effective and useful. Simply stated, performance-evaluation systems that do not focus on results completely miss the corporate objective—and, regrettably, this applies to most of the evaluation systems currently in use.

Ideal Performance Evaluation System

The concept of employee evaluation is to measure each employee's actual performance as compared to planned performance and supervisory feedback on observed behavior. As described, this is the ideal, but rarely the norm, at least in most companies' practical use and application of the method.

Therefore, in order to be an effective measurement, every employee evaluation must contain both an evaluation of the employee's performance at his or her current position and an analysis of the employee's potential to successfully take on greater responsibility. In addition and also as previously described, employee evaluations must always result in development and advancement methods mutually agreed upon by manager and employee.

It is always critical to remember that employee evaluations are not assessments of an individual's personality, character, or traits. That said, of course character and personality issues will influence the evaluation, but they must play a secondary role; they should not be actual evaluation criteria or measures. In other words, the manager (evaluator) is not primarily interested in whether the employee is diligent, organized, detail-oriented, or creative, or if he or she is a self-starter who shows initiative.

To reemphasize the most essential point of the evaluation measurement, the manager's primary purpose here is to assess the employee's achieved results as compared to planned results.

In order to be most effective, employee evaluation should be fluid; it should be both formal and informal. Employees should never feel that the assessment of their performance is a once-a-year-only event. There should be constant feedback between managers and every employee. In addition, a formal evaluation should also take place at regular intervals in order to provide a useful measurement of every employee's actual results versus planned results. (This, in turn, reinforces governance and controls, as described in chapter 4.) As a rule, annual performance evaluations are sufficient, but interim formal evaluations may be necessary for underperforming employees (at management discretion).

Finally, employee evaluations provide an indispensable benefit to managers: feedback on their own effectiveness. Consequently, each time a manager evaluates an employee's performance, the employee should provide the manager with feedback on his or her managerial performance and leadership. Effective managers recognize this and utilize it optimally.

The table below reflects the most-effective evaluation process:

EVALUATION PROCESS

STEP 1	MANAGER AND EMPLOYEE JOINTLY DETERMINE THE GOALS THAT THE EMPLOYEE IS TO ACHIEVE WITHIN THE EVALUATION PERIOD (EMPLOYEE'S TARGET PERFORMANCE).
STEP 2	MANAGER THEN MEASURES THE EMPLOYEE'S ACTUAL PERFORMANCE, AS COMPARED TO THE TARGET PERFORMANCE (MEASUREMENT OF ACTUAL RESULTS ACHIEVED).
STEP 3	MANAGER MEASURES THE DEVIATIONS BETWEEN TARGET PERFORMANCE AND ACTUAL RESULTS. THE KEY QUESTIONS TO ASK ARE: 1. WHICH OBJECTIVES HAVE BEEN ACHIEVED, AND WHICH HAVE NOT? 2. WHAT ARE THE REASONS FOR THE DIFFERENCE BETWEEN TARGET AND ACTUAL VALUES? (NOTE THE SIMILARITY TO THE QUESTIONS ASKED REGARDING GOVERNANCE AND CONTROLS IN CHAPTER 3.)
STEP 4	MANAGER ENGAGES EMPLOYEE IN DIALOGUE, SEEKING FEEDBACK ON MORE- OR LESS-EFFECTIVE BEHAVIOR AS IT APPLIES TO IMPROVING FUTURE RESULTS; EMPLOYEE HAS THE OPPORTUNITY TO PROVIDE ESSENTIAL FEEDBACK TO MANAGER AS WELL (AS DESCRIBED IN THE TEXT PRECEDING THIS TABLE).

Using the process outlined in the table above, every evaluation should assess the following four areas of human dynamics and interrelationships:

- dealing with conflict and ambiguity
- problem solving
- providing advice
- respect for others (including those not present [i.e., "not talking about other people"])

These areas are particularly suitable to evaluating the relational competence of another person, as applies to both the manager's perception of the employee and the employee's perception of the manager.

The following table contains some useful and effective questions for evaluation purposes:

GENERAL PERCEPTIONS

THESE QUESTIONS RELATE TO EACH INDIVIDUAL'S SELF-PERCEPTION, AS WELL AS HIS OR HER PERCEPTIONS OF OTHERS. (AS THE TWO ARE INTERRELATED [FOR MORE INFORMATION ON PERSONALITY BASICS, SEE CHAPTER 1].)

KEY QUESTION # 1	HOW DO I SEE MYSELF, AND HOW DO I SEE THE OTHER PERSON?
KEY QUESTION # 2	HOW DOES THE OTHER PERSON SEE ME, AND HOW DOES HE OR SHE SEE HIMSELF OR HERSELF?

DEALING WITH CONFLICT/AMBIGUITY

DEALING WITH CONTRADICTIONS AND HANDLING AMBIGUOUS SITUATIONS PROVIDE THE CORE OF RELATIONAL COMPETENCE. IF TWO PEOPLE AGREE, IT IS NOT HARD FOR THEM TO COOPERATE. WHEN CONFRONTED WITH AN OPPOSING OR DEVIATING OPINION ON AN ISSUE, AN INDIVIDUAL'S COMMUNICATION SKILLS BECOME APPARENT. THE SAME APPLIES TO DEALING WITH AMBIGUITY AND/OR UNCLEAR SITUATIONS OR INFORMATION. (REMEMBER OUR DISCUSSION OF THE IMPORTANCE OF CLARITY AND LACK OF AMBIGUITY IN RELATION TO GOVERNANCE AND CONTROLS IN CHAPTER 4.)

KEY QUESTION # 1	IS THE OTHER PERSON ILLUSTRATING AN ISSUE IN SUCH A WAY THAT IT IS EASY FOR ME TO LISTEN CALMLY?
KEY QUESTION # 2	DOES THE OTHER PERSON GIVE ME THE SPACE TO ILLUSTRATE MY POINT OF VIEW?
KEY QUESTION # 3	DOES THE OTHER PERSON APPEAR DEFENSIVE, OR DISPLAY OTHER REACTIONS OR ATTITUDES THAT I CAN READILY OBSERVE (COMBATIVENESS, VINDICATION, WITHDRAWAL, COUNTERATTACK, SULKING, ETC.)?
KEY QUESTION # 4	DOES THE OTHER PERSON ACCEPT MY OPINION?
KEY QUESTION # 5	DO MISUNDERSTANDINGS ARISE EASILY BETWEEN US?

KEY QUESTION #6	DO I FEEL FEAR IN RESPONSE TO THE OTHER PERSON'S REACTIONS/ATTITUDE? IF SO, WHAT AM I AFRAID OF? (POSSIBILITIES INCLUDE, BUT ARE NOT LIMITED TO, FEAR OF REJECTION, FEAR OF GIVING IN TOO EASILY/BEING TAKEN ADVANTAGE OF, FEAR OF INABILITY TO EXPRESS ONESELF CLEARLY, ETC.)
KEY QUESTION #7	DO I FEEL THAT THE OTHER PERSON APPRECIATES AND RESPECTS ME, DESPITE THE CRITICISM?
KEY QUESTION #8	DO I FEEL THAT ISSUES BROUGHT FORWARD BY THE OTHER PERSON ARE SOMETIMES UNJUSTIFIED?
KEY QUESTION #9	IS THE ATMOSPHERE FRIENDLY OR HOSTILE?
KEY QUESTION #10	DOES THE OTHER PERSON GIVE ME THE SPACE TO ILLUSTRATE MY POINT OF VIEW?

PROBLEM SOLVING

WHEN PROFESSIONAL ISSUES ARE RESOLVED IN A GROUP, THE DEGREE OF FRICTION IS USUALLY QUITE HIGH. IN ORDER TO ACHIEVE SUCCESSFUL TEAMWORK (COOPERATION AND COLLABORATION), IT IS ESSENTIAL THAT ALL INVOLVED BRING FORWARD THEIR OWN OPINIONS, WHILE REMAINING OPEN TO CONSTRUCTIVE CRITICISM AND SUGGESTIONS.

KEY QUESTION #1	DOES THE OTHER PERSON MAKE SURE THAT EVERYONE HAS UNDERSTOOD HIM OR HER?
KEY QUESTION #2	IS THE OTHER PERSON ABLE TO PRESENT OPINIONS EMPHATICALLY?
KEY QUESTION #3	DOES THE OTHER PERSON LIKE TO ADDRESS OTHER PEOPLE'S SUGGESTIONS BY EITHER INCLUDING OR REBUTTING THEM?
KEY QUESTION #4	IS THE OTHER PERSON WILLING TO PROVIDE BACKGROUND INFORMATION IN ORDER TO BRING OTHERS TO HIS OR HER LEVEL OF KNOWLEDGE?
KEY QUESTION #5	IS THE OTHER PERSON'S PRESENCE A BURDEN OR A RELIEF TO ME?
KEY QUESTION #6	DOES THE OTHER PERSON'S OPTIMISTIC/PESSIMISTIC ATTITUDE AFFECT ME? IF SO, HOW?
KEY QUESTION #7	AM I WILLING TO CONSIDER THE OTHER PERSON'S NEW IDEAS, OR DO I DEFEND MYSELF AGAINST THEM?

PROVIDING ADVICE

THE ADVISOR MUST BE AWARE OF THE FACT THAT THE PERSON SEEKING ADVICE IS RARELY EXPECTING COMPLETE AND CONCRETE SOLUTIONS, BUT SHOULD POSSESS ENOUGH EXPERT KNOWLEDGE TO PROVIDE THE SOUGHT ADVICE. THE ADVISOR SHOULD LET THE OTHER PERSON DETERMINE THE SOLUTION BY HELPING HIM OR HER TO BETTER UNDERSTAND THE PROBLEM AND TO DEVELOP EFFECTIVE APPROACHES FOR DESIGNING USEFUL AND WORKABLE SOLUTIONS.

KEY QUESTION #1	DOES THE OTHER PERSON HELP ME TO DEFINE MY PROBLEM MORE PRECISELY, AND HAS HE OR SHE UNDERSTOOD ME CORRECTLY?
KEY QUESTION #2	DOES IT BECOME APPARENT THAT THE OTHER PERSON HAS AN IDEA OF MY WAY OF SOLVING PROBLEMS?
KEY QUESTION #3	DO I FEEL THAT I AM "DIFFERENT" FROM OTHER PEOPLE? IF SO, IN WHAT WAY(S)?
KEY QUESTION #4	CAN I ASK MY QUESTIONS OPENLY, AND DO I FEEL SECURE THAT THE OTHER PERSON RESPECTS ME AND CONSIDERS MY ISSUE AND POINT OF VIEW SERIOUSLY?
KEY QUESTION #5	DO I FEEL ENCOURAGED AND MOTIVATED, OR INTERROGATED AND INFERIOR?

RESPECT FOR OTHERS

THIS REFERS TO RESPECT FOR OTHER PEOPLE, INCLUDING TALKING ABOUT PEOPLE NOT PRESENT— OR REFUSING TO DO SO. WHAT A PERSON SAYS ABOUT PEOPLE WHO ARE NOT PRESENT GIVES AN IMPRESSION CONCERNING HIS OR HER RESPECT FOR PEOPLE, AS WELL AS THE INFLUENCE OF PERSONS NOT PRESENT.

KEY QUESTION #1	DOES THE OTHER PERSON REFER TO PEOPLE WITH ESTEEM, RESPECT, AND INTEREST, AND DOES HE OR SHE INCLUDE THE SUGGESTIONS OF OTHERS, INCLUDING THOSE NOT PRESENT?
KEY QUESTION #2	DOES THE OTHER PERSON REFER TO OTHERS IN A DERISIVE AND COMPROMISING MANNER, OR DOES HE OR SHE PRAISE AND RESPECT THEM? DOES HE OR SHE TEND TO COMPLAIN ABOUT OTHERS?
KEY QUESTION #3	DOES THE OTHER PERSON TURN TO OTHERS FOR COOPERATION AND TEAMWORK, OR DOES HE OR SHE PREFER TO WORK ALONE, THINKING OTHERS WOULD NOT BE ABLE TO HELP?
KEY QUESTION #4	IS THE OTHER PERSON WILLING TO PROVIDE BACKGROUND INFORMATION TO DEMONSTRATE HOW WELL-INFORMED HE/SHE IS CONCERNING THE PROBLEMS OF OTHERS?
KEY QUESTION #5	WHAT ATMOSPHERE DO I PERCEIVE IN THE OTHER PERSON'S GROUP WHEN HE OR SHE IS PRESENT OR ABSENT?
KEY QUESTION #6	WOULD I APPRECIATE THE OTHER PERSON TALKING ABOUT ME IN THE SAME MANNER?

As a result of the evaluation process (including the use of the questions in the above table), manager and employee should mutually agree on new targets for results. They should also mutually agree on development measures to close the employee's experience and knowledge gaps. Finally, they should agree on options for employee advancement—that is, the employee's potential to take on greater responsibility within the current position. (Remember, advancement and promotion are not one and the same; we will discuss advancement in greater detail later in this chapter.) The manager and the employee should then mutually agree on measures to develop this potential.

To reiterate: in order to make the evaluation measurement as effective as possible, managers should use it as an opportunity to gather feedback on their own performance from employees. Therefore, be sure to use the questions outlined in the table above to obtain employees' responses to your managerial performance, as well as their responses to their own assessed performance.

Basics of Employee Advancement

Remember, companies expect every manager to recognize employees with the talent to take on greater responsibility and to challenge those employees to increase these capabilities.

Employees must be encouraged with respect to both their expert responsibilities and their management/leadership potential. Expert (specialist) advancement usually presents no difficulties, and the path for it is generally organized and easy to understand and follow. The encouragement of management and/or leadership skills is much more difficult, especially for employees currently holding a position without management responsibilities. (Frequently, the current manager/supervisor feels threatened by this and deals with the fear by ignoring this type of skill building.)

Employee advancement is a key managerial responsibility, and failing to develop employees is a sign of an ineffective manager.

The following list outlines some typical opportunities for improving and enhancing managerial/leadership skills:

- representation (standing in for a manager at a meeting)
- project performance
- serving as a team leader, spearheading a committee, leading meetings
- decision-making empowerment, including announcement items (e.g., the manager allows an employee to make a decision that involves companywide or departmental announcement, such as selecting a new candidate for a position)

Again, always remember that advancement and promotion are not synonymous. *Advancement* refers to increased responsibility within the current position held; *promotion* refers to a vertical move to a new position. Having extensively defined and described methods and measurements for employee development and advancement, let's turn our attention to frequent and significant obstacles related to them.

Employee-Development Obstacles

Although there are other obstacles to development, limiting employees' decision-making power is probably the most significant one. In truth, lack of decision-making authority is at the core of most of the other impediments. How many employees in how many companies have too little decision-making authority simply because managers are afraid employees might make the wrong decision?

Not empowering employees to make decisions is a managerial mistake.

Managers tend to forget that their own judgment and problem-solving skills are the direct result of the opportunities they have had to make their own decisions. As previously described, decision making is an experiential process—there is no other way to learn and refine this skill than by making mistakes. This is true for everyone, managers and employees alike. Delegating, strategic planning, governance, controls, and all the tools and techniques previously discussed all hinge on clear and empowered decision making. Simply put, managers cannot just use "lip service": they must empower employees to make decisions, and then step aside so employees can step up—the evaluation process will then provide a useful measurement of the results achieved (as will governance and controls [see chapter 4]).

The issues with decision making notwithstanding, there are other significant obstacles to employee development and advancement. Let's examine the most frequent ones.

Lack of Consistency between Set Goals and Development/ Advancement

If advancement measures are not the result of a comparison of target goals and actual results, followed by the determination of experience and knowledge gaps and the requisite development measures to close those gaps, the manager is wasting company resources—money, talent, or both. Development and advancement must be goal-oriented and must also correspond to areas with responsibility for results or decision-making authority. (Here again we see the linchpin of decision making!)

Overuse of Central Training Departments

Far too often we hear such comments as, "If we can afford a training department, it should fulfill its responsibility to train our people." Such an attitude misses the principle that employee development is one of the most important tasks of every direct superior. It should not and cannot be delegated. The training department can only assist the manager. (This is much the same as our discussion of centralized planning departments in chapter 2. Management tools and techniques are essential to managerial performance.)

Overemphasis of Expert Skills; Underemphasis of Challenging Opportunities

There remains an incongruity between training in expert skills (sales, accounting, materials management, HR administration, machine operation, and even IT) and management skills. Development of management skills should not start with managers who have held their positions for a year or longer; it should start with the upcoming generation that will fill management positions in the future. Opportunities for decision making, problem solving, project management, and other key management tasks should be offered to all employees with the potential to excel in these areas as soon as that potential is determined. Again, the globalization and virtual teams of today's business world make employee development and advance more critical than ever. The days of aspiring to decades-long service with one company are long gone, and employees who do not feel valued and utilized will look for greener pastures.

The foregoing obstacles are crucial to avoid (or at least minimize), but let's also reiterate an obstacle already touched upon: managers should avoid "spontaneous evaluations" in the form of unconstructive criticism or vague comments. Informal evaluation should go on continually, but in the form of productive and purposeful manager/employee dialogues, not offhand comments that provide no meaningful information, especially if made while others are within earshot.

Finally, always remember that employee development and advancement is a key management tool. *Managerial success is measured on increased employee performance, so development impacts both the employee and the manager.* Encourage employees to utilize mentorship as well, as this type of coaching beyond the manager's purview is beneficial to one and all.

Handling Difficult Conversations: Some Tips for More-Productive Development and Advancement Talks

As discussed, managers are expected to conduct development and advancement talks with employees at regular intervals. Although we have touched on much of this earlier in this chapter, it bears repeating. Here are some tips for making those conversations as useful as possible for both managers and employees:

- Development and advancement talks should, as often as possible, refer only to concrete measurable performance and behavior.

- Center the conversations on mutually agreed-up goals (targets) and achieved results, not on employee characteristics or personality traits.
- Allow employees to speak freely, offering their observations on their own behavior and results, as well as yours as the manager.
- Long-term change in behavior (e.g., improved performance on the part of the employee) can only be achieved by an emphasis on successful experiences, not by criticizing mistakes (which the employee perceives as punishment). An employee's past mistakes should only be the object of a development and advancement talk if they can contribute to better performance in the future. The past cannot be changed, so the conversation should be centered on the future 80 percent of the time. (Similar to the 80/20 percent allocation of time to governance [future] and controls [past] explained in chapter 4.)
- Development and advancement talks should have a motivating effect. The manager should try to understand the employee's needs in order to satisfy them, as long as this corresponds to the primary needs of the company. (We will discuss motivation in greater detail in chapter 7.)
- Employee evaluations should not be judgmental; nor should be they put the employee on the defensive or offensive. Examples of things the manager should *not* say:

    - "You should try harder ..."
    - "You never manage to ..."
    - "I have told you more than a dozen times to ..."
    - "In the future, please ..."
    - "Considering your previous education, I would have expected more ..."
    - "All in all I am satisfied, but ..."

- Reject attempts by the employee to "back delegate" during the course of development and advancement talks. Employees' development is not furthered by having someone (the manager or anyone else) make decisions for them. Instead, they must be empowered to make decisions and given the appropriate support to follow through effectively.

- Development and advancement talks should be separate from salary-increase discussions, as the performance is only one of several criteria for the determination of compensation. (However, it makes sense to have the development and advancement talks prior to meetings in which salaries are discussed. In many companies, governance specifies a grid, so performance evaluations make the salary percentage increase self-evident. This is efficient, as it avoids the necessity of multiple meetings.)

- As stated, the development and advancement talks are also an opportunity to evaluate the manager's performance. Don't miss this opportunity! Ask the employee, "What have I done or not done that has interfered with your performance? What should I do or not do in the future to increase your effectiveness?" If you have made mistakes, step up to them. Model the accountability you expect from employees.

Above all, always keep this in mind: increased employee performance is the key measure of managerial skill. Effective managers never underestimate the importance of employee development and advancement.

Applying What You Have Learned

As the core statement opening this chapter emphasizes, and as we have reiterated throughout, a manager's skill is best measured by increased employee performance. Therefore, all managers must transcend obstacles to employee development and advancement, face and overcome their own fears of relinquishing decision-making authority, and avail themselves of the opportunity to increase their own performance through employee feedback.

Here are some essential steps related to employee development and advancement that we all need to implement:

1. Utilize the key management tool of employee development and advancement, including effective methods and measurements (continual dialoguing with employees, plus a formal evaluation

system). Like the rest of the management tool kit, employee development and advancement must never be delegated.

2. Empower employees to make decisions and provide the necessary support to allow them to do so with confidence and effectiveness.

3. Establish the clear differences between development and advancement, and between advancement and promotion, and encourage employees to seek and obtain mentorship, as appropriate.

By incorporating the above items 1 through 3 into our daily routine, we are well on the way to becoming effective managers. And that's "simply management"!

Now that we've thoroughly discussed employee development and advancement, let's turn to another key management tool: communication, which we will explore in the next chapter.

6

COMMUNICATION

Effective communication is strategic: it determines exactly who is to receive what information, when, how, and with what intention.

Definition of Communication

Communication refers to the exchange of messages that convey information, ideas, attitudes, emotions, opinions, or instructions; such exchanges can be between individuals or groups. Regardless of who is involved in the exchanges, the primary goal of communication is always to understand and/or coordinate thoughts or activities among the people concerned. *Information* refers to the passing on of knowledge from one person to another.

In terms of its application as a management tool, communication is the transfer of information from a sender to a receiver for the purpose of achieving goals. As such, communication is essential to the effective operation of every organization. (Previous chapters have already described the ways in which communication, as an essential component of the management tool kit, works in concert with other key tools and techniques, such as strategic planning and goal setting, organizational structure, governance and controls, and employee development.)

The true-to-life business scenario that follows illustrates effective methods of communication: precise determination of who is to receive what information, when, how, and with what intention. Let's examine how the use of strategic communication empowers rich relationships and dynamic interactions in the twenty-first-century workplace.

(**NOTE:** *Although a key management tool, communication must be cascaded appropriately to all levels, and employees must communicate effectively with one another and with management. Therefore, much of the content in this chapter applies to managers and nonmanagers.*)

True-to-Life Business Scenario: Effective Methods of Strategic Communication

Pamela is a project manager responsible for the implementation of new global call center software. This software was supposed to be implemented globally last year, but most sites did not follow the process and did not move to the new software. The project was considered a failure. The company has decided to relaunch the project.

The call center software implementation is one of Pamela's performance goals. Pamela is concerned about the project's success globally because the company does not yet have buy-in from all the regions. (And implementation already failed when initiated last year.) Accordingly, Pamela has asked for guidance from Roberto, a global communications specialist. Roberto asked Pamela for a communication plan, and she shared the original communication plan from the initial failed project. This original plan consisted of one manager alignment meeting, followed by three e-mails that were several pages long. Each e-mail outlined a twelve-step process for "going live" with the software, including supporting details on the process.

After looking at the original plan, Roberto shared with Pamela some very important things to remember when communicating in a global organization:

1. Communication by itself does not ensure a successful implementation, but a lack of communication will lead to an unsuccessful implementation.

2. Clear and effective communication takes time and planning. A communication plan should include bite-size, digestible messages disseminated over a period of time. The communication should begin with high-level (broad and overarching) messages that become more specific over time.

Roberto further explained that one of the most common mistakes in this area is creating long, detailed communications. When someone opens a text-heavy e-mail or document, it is easy to put it aside to read later—but, more often than not, later never comes. Communication that goes unread is not effective. It is far more effective to start with a brief, high-level overview message. Follow-up messages can then refer back to that original high-level overview message, reemphasizing key points without repeating all the information.

In addition to his suggestions on the communication method described above, Roberto recommended using a spreadsheet to create a strategic communication plan with the following information:

- **key message**—main reason for the communication
- **audience**—individuals/groups who will receive the communication
- **content owner**—individual(s) responsible for creating the communication
- **delivery owner**—appropriate individual(s) to send (or communicate) the message to
- **vehicle**—best method to deliver the message (meeting, e-mail, poster, town hall, etc.)
- **delivery date**—when to deliver the message
- **status**—how to keep track of each message (i.e., status of each communication)

Roberto also gave Pamela some tips for creating more-effective communications:

- Analyze the content to identify bite-size chunks.

- Ensure that the first sentence of every communication is the most important point (action required, due date, reason why the communication is important).
- Think about timing for each message; reemphasize important information more than once, but avoid unnecessary repetition.
- Messages should be as clear and concise as possible; take time to craft all messages.
- Carefully consider who delivers the message. (Even if you are the person responsible for drafting the communication, it may be more effective to have someone else deliver it; for example, the manager of the team should communicate to the team.)
- Don't assume messages will automatically be cascaded through an organization! Put them in the communication plan.

The table that follows shows the first page of Pamela's new strategic communication plan. The complete plan would be far too detailed to re-create here, but the sample below reflects how Pamela used the tips and recommendations that Roberto shared with her.

STRATEGIC COMMUNICATION PLAN

AUDIENCE	MESSAGES	CONTENT OWNER	DELIVERY OWNER	VEHICLE	STATUS	DELIVERY DATE
REGIONAL SITE MANAGERS	ANNOUNCE PROJECT KICKOFF	PAMELA	GLOBAL CALL CENTER VP	E-MAIL	COMPLETED	MAY 4
REGIONAL SITE MANAGERS	INTRODUCTION OF PROJECT MANAGER	PAMELA	GLOBAL CALL CENTER VP	E-MAIL	COMPLETED	MAY 10
REGIONAL SITE MANAGERS	ANNOUNCE HIGH-LEVEL PROJECT GOALS	PAMELA	PAMELA	CALENDAR INVITE	COMPLETED	MAY 13
REGIONAL SITE MANAGERS	INVITATION TO WEBEX TO COVER PROJECT PLAN	PAMELA	PAMELA	WEBEX	IN PROGRESS	MAY 19
REGIONAL SITE MANAGERS	PROJECT TIMELINE	PAMELA	PAMELA	E-MAIL	IN PROGRESS	MAY 19
CALL CENTER MANAGERS	MEETING MINUTES	PAMELA	REGIONAL SITE MANAGER	SITE MEETING	IN PROGRESS	MAY 25
CALL CENTER MANAGERS	PROJECT ANNOUNCEMENT	PAMELA	REGIONAL SITE MANAGER	SITE MEETING	IN PROGRESS	MAY 25

Pamela spent a great deal of time up front thinking about communication, and she sought expert advice on how to craft the most-effective plan. As a result, her communications were clear, strategic, and purposeful. The final complete strategic communication plan (not shown here) incorporated all the advice and recommendations that Pamela received from Roberto. By using an effective plan, Pamela avoided the issues that caused the initial launch to fail. The project was successfully implemented, and Pamela met her performance goal.

As we can see in the above scenario, following the tips for effective communication leads to success for employees, managers, and organizations. To reemphasize our core statement: *effective communication is always strategic, determining exactly who is to receive what information, when, how, and with what intention.*

Let's turn our attention to the best ways to apply that governing principle to contemporary communication.

Twenty-First-Century Communication

The technology of the Information Age has brought about many changes all over the world. One of the areas that has seen the most-extensive changes is communication. The telephone and international mail service have enabled global communication for a very long time, but technological advances in the latter part of the twentieth century and continuing into the twenty-first mean that communications are still changing and will continue to change. This applies to both the methods and speed of communication. For example, we once waited days or weeks for what we now call "snail mail"; we then became accustomed to waiting an hour or for several minutes to receive a fax, and then a few minutes or just seconds to receive an e-mail. The invention of instant messaging and texting has enabled even faster two-way communication. Sometimes it feels like we can't type fast enough during these type of exchanges. The changes are rapid, and keeping pace requires flexibility and speed. And that's just where written communication is concerned. In terms of spoken communication, we have gone from one-on-one telephone calls, to large group conference calls, to video conferences on laptops, to instant video conferences on smartphones, anywhere and at any time.

It would seem that all these technological advances would make business communication simple, in terms of both global and virtual workplaces. Nothing could be further from the truth. Communication today is far from simple. Technology enables speed and convenience, but with speed and convenience also comes the ability to quickly send miscommunications. Texting and e-mail do not allow the reader to see facial expressions or hear tone of voice. The absence of these clues can lead to miscommunication. In addition, people often send messages without carefully editing to ensure clarity and/or avoid misinterpretation of tone (e.g., by the use of capital letters or exclamation points). In short, there are many challenges to effective communication in contemporary business, with countless opportunities for miscommunication—no matter how unintended they might be.

Remember that strategic communication always considers the who, what (information and intention), when, and how of every exchange. Therefore, in order for communication to be effective, the message received must be the same as the message sent. Anything else is miscommunication.

Technology and Effective Communication

The tips listed below can help ensure effective, meaningful communication in our fast-paced, electronically dominated business world (note that these tie in with and expand upon the tips included in the true-to-life business scenario at the beginning of this chapter):

- Carefully review all texts and e-mails before sending.
- Ask others to review a draft of your message to ensure clarity.
- When using e-mail, carefully check the "to" field to make sure you are sending the message to the correct person(s). (This is especially true when forwarding!)

- Don't include people in meetings, calls, or messages unless the content or discussion truly impacts them, will result in action items for them, contains information they need to know, or offers them an opportunity to add value through their input, feedback, or presence.
- Don't use e-mail or text as a means of avoiding what should be a face-to-face conversation (or at least a phone call or video conference). If you have to respond to an e-mail or text more than a few times, pick up the phone or schedule a face-to-face meeting. (In terms of global and virtual workplaces, this can sometimes be challenging, if not impossible. Video conferences/chats should be used to substitute for face-to-face meetings in such instances.)
- Keep e-mail messages short and to the point. People are less likely to read long e-mails.
- Clearly state what you want or need so the receiver does not wonder about what to do with the information. (For example, do you want the receiver to do something with the information in the e-mail? If so, specify the requested action. Similarly, if the e-mail is just for information, specify that as well.) Everyone is busy, and the time and energy wasted on guesswork do not benefit anyone—or the company.
- Ensure that the first sentence is the most important one in the message. The reader may not read beyond that point. This is especially true if the receiver is reading e-mail on a smartphone with limited screen space.

Needless to say, the ability to compose efficient and effective e-mails is an extremely useful skill in terms of both productivity and relationship dynamics. As with all communication exchanges, the main goal where e-mail is concerned is to achieve the desired outcome (intent of/reason for the e-mail) while simultaneously respecting the time and perspective of the other person (e-mail recipient). The tips listed above should assist us in achieving that goal, and there are also many online articles and blog posts that offer similar advice and suggestions. Below is a table of key points on how to write effective e-mails; feel free to share it with colleagues and employees alike.

E-MAIL ESSENTIALS

Do's	Don'ts
DO STATE YOUR POINT CLEARLY AND QUICKLY.	DON'T RAMBLE, GIVE UNNECESSARY INFORMATION, OR WASTE TIME WITH LONG INTRODUCTIONS.
DO CLEARLY SPECIFY ANY ACTIONS OR RESPONSES NEEDED.	DON'T LEAVE THE RECIPIENT(S) GUESSING AS TO THE POINT OR INTENT OF THE E-MAIL, OR WHAT ACTIONS ARE REQUIRED.
DO USE A CLEAN FORMAT AND EASY-TO-READ FONT.	DON'T USE FANCY BACKGROUNDS, COLORS, OR FONTS.
DO EDIT/PROOFREAD TO MAKE SURE YOUR E-MAIL IS CONCISE, CLEAR, AND EASY TO UNDERSTAND.	DON'T USE AMBIGUOUS LANGUAGE OR COMPLICATED TERMINOLOGY; (IF TECHNICAL MATERIAL, ENSURE THE RECIPIENT POSSESSES THE NECESSARY EXPERT KNOWLEDGE PRIOR TO SENDING).
DO ASK SOMEONE ELSE TO PROOFREAD A DRAFT BEFORE SENDING IF YOU ARE UNSURE OF THE CLARITY OF YOUR CONTENT.	DON'T SEND THE E-MAIL IF YOU ARE UNSURE ABOUT ITS CLARITY OR TONE.
DO BE COURTEOUS, PROFESSIONAL, AND PERSONABLE.	DON'T USE LANGUAGE, TONE, OR STYLE THAT COULD IN ANY WAY APPEAR UNPROFESSIONAL, DISCOURTEOUS, OR OFFENSIVE.

(Some of the suggestions in the above table were adapted from "Fifteen Tips for Writing Effective E-mail" on the website *Think Simple Now*.[3])

Global Teams and Effective Communication

Working in a global company means coworkers are located in many different time zones. It is not uncommon to have project team members scattered around the globe. When team members have twelve-hour time differences, team meetings are more difficult. Scheduling a few calls in the middle of the night for one or more team members might work on occasion, but it is not feasible long-term.

Project teams need to find ways to collaborate (this applies to both global and virtual teamwork). Teams that plan well take advantage of the time difference to keep work rolling around the clock, but that takes planning and clear communication. (Again, this is also true of teams with telecommuters.) If someone in North America passes work off to a

---

[3] "Fifteen Tips for Writing Effective E-mail," *Think Simple Now*, http://thinksimplenow.com/productivity/15-tips-for-writing-effective-email/.

teammate in Asia with clear instructions, it is possible to be more efficient and effective than a team in a single location. However, sending the same work with little or no clear communication about what needs to be done means the project will be stalled, and the person on the receiving end will be frustrated—or even worse, will try to muddle through and end up doing work that results in revisions or work done more than once.

The following tips can help ensure effective, meaningful communication and cooperation in global work environments:

- Be aware of cultural differences, and research the culture of the countries where team members are based.
- Avoid meeting times that will result in any team members having to participate in the middle of the night. Consider alternate work hours for periods of time when overlap in business hours are required, or rotate the meeting time in order to ensure that everyone takes a turn with the inconvenient late-night call.
- Have a clear project plan, and clearly state which time zone you are using when communicating deadlines.
- Document procedures for work that will be done in more than one location in order to ensure consistency.
- Keep a team calendar that includes holidays in each country. Plan ahead based on holidays.
- Use video conferencing if possible.
- Speak slowly and clearly, especially when on the phone.
- Provide agendas and written minutes for all meetings.
- Record virtual meetings for those who cannot attend in person.
- Utilize web conferencing to share presentations during meetings.
- Meet in person when possible.

Virtual Teams and Effective Communication

As stated, many of the tips on effective global communication also apply to virtual workplaces. Certainly the suggestions for integrating technology into effective communication pertains to virtual teams, as such situations would be impossible without technology. Use any and all pertinent suggestions in the preceding sections when dealing with virtual-team situations.

In addition, the list below includes some tips that are especially useful for virtual teams and telecommuting employees:[4]

- Make it a priority to have regular face-to-face meetings (once a month or at least once a quarter).
- Apprise virtual team members of all pertinent onsite goings-on in order to ensure they feel as valued as in-house team members.
- During video conferences, speak as if all attendees are physically at the meeting.
- Discourage texting and instant messaging by meeting participants. Every attendee's focus should be on the meeting, not on tangential conversations.
- Encourage virtual team members to resolve conflicts face-to-face if possible, or via video conferencing/chat if not possible. Phone calls are not an optimal vehicle for conflict resolution, but are preferable to e-mails or texts.

Now that we have explored the main areas of twenty-first-century communication as it pertains to business—technology, global organizations, and virtual teams—let's turn our attention to communication methods and how to ensure that we always choose the right method for every message.

Choosing the Right Method of Communication

For the most part, the business situation at hand will dictate the best method to use. Global organizations and virtual teams need to maximize effective use of video conferencing but must never underestimate the importance of face-to-face interaction. Every company needs to have meetings where employees can interact in person.

---

[4] "Communication: Various Best Practices Research," http://onlinemba.unc .edu/research-and-insights/developing-real-skills-for-virtual-teams/ virtual-team-challenges/.

Technology must never take the place of one-on-one communication.

Nevertheless, technology does much to facilitate business communication. Telephone conversations, conference calls, and video conferences do enable global business. Texts and e-mails make it possible to send and receive information rapidly, and e-mails are a good way to recap the content of phone conversations—especially when other individuals who were not on the call need to be in the loop. These qualifiers can help determine the best method to use. (Also refer to the tips and recommendations included in the true-to-life business scenario at the beginning of this chapter.)

COMMUNICATION GOALS

GOAL OF COMMUNICATION	TIME SENSITIVITY	BEST METHOD TO USE
TAKE ACTION ON INFORMATION	ASAP	E-MAIL OR PHONE; FACE-TO-FACE (IF POSSIBLE)
RELAY INFORMATION	NONE	E-MAIL LABELED "INFORMATION ONLY"
PROBLEM RESOLUTION	URGENT	FACE-TO-FACE (IF NOT POSSIBLE, PHONE CALL)
CONFLICT RESOLUTION	URGENT	FACE-TO-FACE (IF NOT POSSIBLE, PHONE CALL OR VIDEO CONFERENCE/CHAT)

We've already discussed that it's always appropriate to reemphasize important information; frequently, it's often critical to do so. So now let's review the guidelines for effective communication, including the key principles and common pitfalls to avoid. (Again, much of this appears in the foregoing sections, and what follows in subsequent sections will serve to reinforce it.)

Of course, the overarching wisdom to observe in all communicative exchanges is simple. Effective communication is strategic: it determines exactly who is to receive what information, when, how, and with what intention.

Communication Guidelines

Principles of Communication

The principles of communication for the sender have a certain priority over those for the receiver, as the sender plays the active role in the communication process, and is therefore responsible for the success of the communication. (The receiver plays a passive role, but, as we've discussed, when the receiver and sender interpret the same message differently, the result is miscommunication.)

It is the sender's responsibility to take the following steps, which must be part of every successful communication:

- planning the communication (who, what [information and intention], when, and how)
- timing of the communication (when to send and when response is due, if applicable)
- establishing delivery (person and vehicle)
- crafting a purposeful, concise, and unambiguous message in order to avoid misinterpretation and/or vague reactions

Again, the above list reinforces and reemphasizes the points already stated. Our discussion thus far has centered on the sender, who bears more responsibility because he or she plays the active role in the communication exchange. However, let's now discuss the other key participant in communication: the receiver.

While it is true that the receiver's role is passive, it is equally true that there is no real communication event without him or her. Communication is an exchange, so it can only occur if there is a sender (speaker or writer) and a receiver (listener or reader). The most important responsibility of the receiver is to focus. The following list specifies what every receiver must do in order for communication to be effective:

- Listen (or read) with full attention and concentration.
- Perceive with an open mind, striving to remain objective and avoid emotional reactions.

- Evaluate the message (and/or any of its components).
- React to the message, either by speaking or writing a reply (note that by completing this last step, the receiver becomes a sender).

Common Pitfalls among Senders

- ineffective or inappropriate wording, which exhibits ambiguous expression of thoughts or ideas
- lack of an effective, strategic communication plan
- disorganized thoughts, which transmit unclear messages and/or miscommunications
- "information overload" (too many different ideas clutter the core message); fills messages with ideas that are not interconnected; all this makes it difficult for the receiver to summarize the information
- inappropriate or ineffective timing when sending messages

Common Pitfalls among Receivers

- appearing unsure of appropriate response, so says nothing in order to avoid conflict or awkward "fallout"
- misinterpretation of intention (this also means the sender was unclear or ambiguous)
- lack of the necessary expert (specialist) knowledge on topic (receiver isn't qualified)
- lack of comprehension (receiver doesn't understand)
- lack of motivation (receiver does not want to participate in exchange)
- focusing more on framing response than on listening carefully
- concentrating on tangential details rather than the main message(s)

Ensuring effective, optimal communication is a key management responsibility. Always follow the guiding principles of who, what (information and intention), when, and how.

Communication Plans

As we saw in the true-to-life business scenario at the beginning of this chapter, communication plans are crucial. A strategic communication plan can lead to the success (or failure) of any project. In addition, lack of effective, strategic communications can lead to all kinds of problems within an organization—even companywide failure.

Following Roberto's insightful advice and recommendations (see true-to-life business scenario), the table below captures the key components of effective, strategic communication plans.

KEY COMPONENTS OF EFFECTIVE/STRATEGIC COMMUNICATION PLANS

AUDIENCE	KEY MESSAGE(S)
CONTENT OWNER	DELIVERY OWNER
VEHICLE	DELIVERY DATE
STATUS	ESSENTIAL DETAILS (ANYTHING OUTSIDE THE KEY COMPONENTS THAT PERTAINS TO A SPECIFIC PLAN AND THAT MUST BE TRACKED)

Communication as a Management Tool

As stated in the note at the beginning of this chapter, much of the descriptions and explanations in this chapter apply equally to the communications of managers and nonmanagers alike. Effective communication is essential for every member of every organization. However, it is the manager's responsibility to ensure that all information is stated or written correctly and that it is distributed in a timely manner to all those who need to receive it, both within and outside the management triangle.

As the manager is responsible for his or her triangle, the internal flow of information is of fundamental importance; the flow of information within the organization, but outside the triangle, is important but not as critical. It is always easier to control our own communication; the communications of others, whether subordinates, peers, or superiors can (and often does) present challenges.

Managers must do their utmost to minimize these challenges as much as possible and must do everything in their power to ensure that communication is fluid, concise, purposeful, and unambiguous.

Given all the aspects of communication (global organizations, virtual teams, and technological advances) that we have considered in this chapter, it is easy to see why it is such an essential management tool—and why so many of the other essential management tools hinge on it. If we cannot communicate with optimal effectiveness, we cannot work with maximal effectiveness. It's as simple as that.

Successful managers know that effective communication must be strategic, determining and reflecting exactly who is to receive what information, when, how, and with what intention. This is how effective managers communicate with employees, peers, and senior management.

Applying What You Have Learned

As the core statement opening this chapter emphasizes, effective communication must always be strategic, determining exactly who is to receive what information, when, how, and with what intention. Managers (and nonmanagers) must avoid miscommunication and must quickly correct any errors in communication that might occur. In the contemporary business world of global and virtual teams, as well as constantly changing technology and telecommunications, this is as challenging as it is imperative.

Here are some essential steps related to communication that we all need to implement:

1. Utilize the key management tool of communication to ensure that all information and messages are concise, purposeful, and unambiguous. Like the rest of the management tool kit, communication is an essential tool that all managers must use to optimal effect. (Strategic communication plans, e-mail guidelines, global communication guidelines, and other best-practice methods assist in ensuring that information flows smoothly and efficiently.)
2. Empower employees to be effective communicators, and provide the necessary support to allow them to do so (using the methods listed above, as well as any others that prove beneficial, useful, and effective).
3. Establish communication guidelines and expectations, and cascade them appropriately to all levels within each management triangle and the organization as a whole.

By incorporating the above items 1 through 3 into our daily routine, we are well on the way to becoming effective managers. And that's "simply management"!

Now that we've thoroughly discussed employee communication, let's turn to the final key management tool: motivation, which we will explore in the next chapter.

7

MOTIVATION

If the manager wants to positively influence or change the behavior of his employee, there is only one starting point: determining what motivates the employee.

Definition of Motivation

Motivation refers to the creation of elements and/or working environments that enable and encourage employees to perform optimally and with maximum effectiveness and efficiency, all in the team-oriented pursuit of organizational success. Although once widely viewed as a "special power" that allows managers to get direct reports to achieve their goals/targets, motivation is now more commonly viewed as management's creation of an organizational climate and culture that addresses the needs of employees. In addition, most motivational models and methodologies now recognize that one person (manager) cannot really motivate others (employees); however, effective managers can and must create environments and conditions that foster self-motivation among employees.

In terms of its application as a management tool in today's business world, motivation is the effective manager's means of encouraging employee self-motivation. Therefore, motivation is essential to the effective operation of every organization because it leads to successful results that are solid and sustainable. (Motivation, an essential component of the management tool kit, works in concert with other key tools and techniques, such as communication, strategic planning and goal setting, organizational structure, governance and controls, and employee development, as we have seen throughout the previous chapters.)

The true-to-life business scenario that follows will illustrate how and why determining what motivates employees is the only way to effectively change or influence their behavior, as well as the most effective way to achieve positive, sustainable results—especially in today's business environment of advanced technology, globalization, and virtual teams.

True-to-Life Business Scenario: Effective Methods of Motivating Employees

AMV Global, an international, multimillion-dollar technology company, learned through an annual employee engagement survey that managers were using outdated and antiquated practices to motivate direct reports. The company was concerned about its employee retention, especially among its high-potential and early career employees. According to the data from the engagement survey, managers and supervisors were using ineffective tactics, such as fear, in an attempt to motivate employees to perform. The problem with this approach was that fear destroyed the employees' trust and respect, ultimately becoming a demotivator.

In addition to utilizing fear, managers had another common approach to motivation: the lure of incentives. This was problematic because the positive behavior and/or improved performance were not sustainable: both ceased as soon as the employees received the promised reward(s). For example, when safety incidents increased, managers would offer rewards for fewer incidents. When the group achieved the goal and the rewards were given, a rise in safety incidents would return. As a result, utilizing the threat of punishment did not impact behavior positively or create sustainable results. Employees knew there would not be lasting consequences from either punishment or reward, so neither one served as an effective motivator.

AMV Global conducted extensive research and found a methodology that complemented the culture it wanted to create. The principle of this methodology is simple but powerful: managers alone cannot motivate employees; motivation is primarily internal to the individual. Managers and supervisors can create an environment in which employees can cultivate their own self-motivation, which can then be sustainable without the use of such short-term influencers as fear and incentives.

The methodology focuses on three components:

1. **Focused Work**—knowing that your work is important and contributes to the organization's mission
    *   Examples include clear expectations, regular feedback, minimal distractions, and sufficient resources to get the job done.
2. **Interpersonal Support**—being able to count on the support of others
    *   Examples include a harmonious and trustworthy environment, and a high degree of collaboration and teamwork.
3. **Individual Value**—having the power to manage your own work
    *   Examples include empowerment to use your own approaches and ideas, authority to make decisions and manage your own work, and the opportunity to develop on the job.

After identifying the model they wanted to use, AMV Global's next step involved training all managers on the new methodology. The success of this project was critical because AMV Global had one hundred high-potential employees in a three-year leadership development program (LDP). Most of the participants were early on in their careers and expected to progress at a reasonable pace. Retention of the LDP employees was a project objective.

In order to support the changes in how managers would help motivate employees, AMV Global created a mentoring program. One of the participants, Pekka, an account manager in Germany and part of the LDP, expressed interest in managing high-level cross-functional projects to his manager, Inga. Inga and Pekka mapped several high-level global projects that involved engineering, marketing, and IT. Inga facilitated buy-in from the other functions to support Pekka on his project. Pekka was excited about the opportunity to collaborate with other groups and had a clear understanding about what the goals and objectives were. Inga created an environment that fostered the three key components of the motivational model: focused work, interpersonal support, and individual value. Inga's management style and the environment she created inspired Pekka.

Management at AMV Global monitored the successful implementation of motivational best practices via future engagement surveys (every twelve months) and focus group meetings (every six months). As a result, participants' survey data showed a favorable improvement in employee engagement, manager effectiveness, and employee retention.

As the above business scenario clearly shows, using effective motivational methods leads to improved results—for employees, managers, and the company. By giving employees the opportunity to cultivate their own natural (internal) motivation, companies create successes that are meaningful and sustainable (as opposed to the less-significant gains resulting from short-term influences like fear and incentives). The ability to use and benefit from this methodology stems from managers' recognizing that determining what motivates employees is the only way to effectively change or positively influence their behavior, as the core statement opening this chapter reveals. Effective managers always recognize this and utilize the technique optimally.

Motivation is a key responsibility of management and an essential management tool. Remember, managers who want to change or influence employee behavior must start by determining what motivates their employee(s).

Motivation Models

Many motivational models and theories exist, and most apply to effective methods of management. For our purposes, the three that are most useful are Abraham Maslow's, Frederick Herzberg's, and Daniel Pink's. Let's explore the motivational models of each of these three theories one by one in order to see how to apply them to our goal of positively impacting employee behavior by determining what motivates employees.

Abraham Maslow's Model

Abraham Maslow had a profound influence on management theory in the twentieth century. The basis of Maslow's theory is the hierarchy of needs. Usually shown as a pyramid (see figure 7-1), with the most-basic needs at the base and the more-advanced needs at the top, this model focuses on the following (in descending order to match the pyramid's structure):

- **self-actualization** (need for and fulfillment of highest potential)
- **esteem** (need for and realization of self-esteem and self-respect)
- **love and belonging** (need for family, friends, and intimacy; attainment of positive relationships)
- **safety and security** (need for personal and financial security, as well as good health and well-being; creation of a "safety net" to guard against accidents, illness, and other negative experiences)
- **physiological needs** (basic biological needs necessary for human survival)

Figure 7-1: Maslow's Hierarchy of Needs

A detailed discussion of Maslow's theories would be beyond the scope and intention of this book. What we as managers need to concern ourselves with is that as individuals progress through life, they learn to respond and react based upon how well they are able to meet each successive level of needs (or how well their primary caregivers have met those needs in the case of their fundamental development).

(**NOTE:** *Image of hierarchy of needs pyramid and explanatory text adapted from standard descriptions of Maslow's motivational theory.*)

Managers must always determine what motivates employees in order to influence or change their behavior with positive and sustainable results.

Practical Application of the Maslow Model

Below are some ideas for how management can use the Maslow model to create a motivating workplace environment. (However, remember, managers' role in this is to foster employee self-motivation, not to attempt to motivate through fear, incentives, or other short-term practices that are not sustainable, as seen in the true-to-life business scenario at the beginning of this chapter.)

Using the Maslow model, each employee's personal growth and development is essential to organizational success. Therefore, managers must strive to identify individual employee needs as a way to promote job satisfaction. It follows that if managers do this, employees will progress toward self-actualization (top of Maslow pyramid [see figure 7-1]), positively impacting the company in the process.

Keeping in mind what we have already established (that managers should foster an environment that encourages employee self-motivation), the table below highlights some key ways that managers can incorporate Maslow's needs into their motivational methodology (again, in descending order to match the pyramid in figure 7-1):

SELF-ACTUALIZATION NEEDS

CREATE AN ENVIRONMENT THAT ENCOURAGES EMPLOYEES TO REACH THEIR HIGHEST POTENTIAL.
EMPOWER EMPLOYEES TO PARTICIPATE IN SETTING GOALS AND MAKING DECISIONS.
PROVIDE OPPORTUNITIES AND SUPPORT FOR EMPLOYEE DEVELOPMENT AND ADVANCEMENT.
ENCOURAGE EMPLOYEES TO BROADEN THEIR EXPERIENCE AND EXPOSURE (THROUGH JOB ROTATION, MENTORSHIP, ETC.).
OFFER OPTIMAL INNOVATIVE AND RISK-TAKING OPPORTUNITIES.
PROVIDE CHALLENGING INTERNAL AND EXTERNAL PROFESSIONAL DEVELOPMENT OPPORTUNITIES.
ENSURE SUPPORTIVE LEADERSHIP THAT ENCOURAGES A HIGH DEGREE OF SELF-CONTROL.
PROVIDE COMPENSATION THAT REFLECTS REWARD FOR EXCEPTIONAL PERFORMANCE.

SELF-ESTEEM NEEDS

CREATE AN ENVIRONMENT THAT ENCOURAGES EMPLOYEES TO RESPECT AND VALUE THEMSELVES AND OTHERS.

INCLUDE EMPLOYEES IN GOAL-SETTING AND DECISION-MAKING PROCESSES, WITH AN APPROPRIATE AMOUNT OF EMPOWERMENT (NOT AS MUCH AS EMPLOYEES READY FOR SELF-ACTUALIZATION).

OFFER OPPORTUNITIES TO BEST USE EXISTING SKILLS AND TALENTS AND TO ACQUIRE NEW ONES.

PROVIDE CLEAR SYMBOLS OF RECOGNITION (E.G., BUSINESS CARDS, NAMES/TITLES LISTED ON COMPANY WEBSITE, IN E-MAIL SIGNATURES, ETC.)

OFFER OPPORTUNITIES FOR COACHING AND DEVELOPMENT (THROUGH MANAGEMENT PROCESS AND MENTORSHIP).

GIVE POSITIVE REINFORCEMENT.

PROVIDE APPROPRIATE VISIBLE "PERKS" (E.G., OFFICE SIZE AND LOCATION, PARKING SPACES, EMPLOYEE-OF-THE-MONTH PROGRAM, ETC.).

ENCOURAGE PARTICIPATION IN THE COMPANY MENTOR PROGRAM.

PROVIDE COMPENSATION THAT REFLECTS RECOGNITION OF PROFESSIONAL GROWTH.

BELONGINGNESS NEEDS

CREATE AN ENVIRONMENT WITH A POSITIVE SOCIAL BASE, WHERE EMPLOYEES FEEL THAT THEY "BELONG" AND ARE APPRECIATED.

ENCOURAGE TEAMWORK AND COLLABORATION.

DISTRIBUTE JOB-SATISFACTION SURVEYS ON A REGULAR BASIS AND VISIBLY USE THE INFORMATION COLLECTED FROM THEM.

SPONSOR COMPANY MEETINGS FOR BOTH BUSINESS AND SOCIAL PURPOSES.

PROVIDE CLOSE PERSONAL LEADERSHIP.

ENCOURAGE EMPLOYEES TO PARTICIPATE IN PROFESSIONAL AND COMMUNITY GROUPS.

INCLUDE TEAM PERFORMANCE AS A MEASUREMENT THAT TIES TO COMPENSATION.

SECURITY NEEDS

CREATE AN ENVIRONMENT WHERE EMPLOYEES FEEL EMOTIONALLY SAFE AND SECURE. (THIS IS IN ADDITION TO THE PHYSICAL SAFETY ENSURED BY PROVIDING FOR BASIC PHYSIOLOGICAL NEEDS.)
REQUIRE ALL EMPLOYEES TO FOLLOW AND OBSERVE ALL SAFETY RULES AND REGULATIONS.
MINIMIZE LAYOFFS AND DOWNSIZING.
PROVIDE WELL-DEFINED JOB DESCRIPTIONS.
AVOID USING INCENTIVES AND/OR THREATENING BEHAVIOR (I.E., USING INCENTIVES AND/OR FEAR AS MOTIVATORS).
GIVE EMPLOYEES INFORMATION ABOUT THE COMPANY'S FINANCIAL STATUS AND FORECASTS ON A REGULAR BASIS.
LET EMPLOYEE COMPENSATION MATCH VALUE PROVIDED, STIPULATING THAT INCREASED PERFORMANCE WILL RESULT IN INCREASED COMPENSATION.

PHYSIOLOGICAL NEEDS

CREATE AN ENVIRONMENT THAT ADDRESSES BASIC NEEDS AND ALLOWS EMPLOYEES TO FEEL PHYSICALLY SAFE AND SECURE.
PROVIDE A CLEAN, SAFE, PLEASANT, AND COMFORTABLE ENVIRONMENT.
GIVE EVERY EMPLOYEE A SALARY IN KEEPING WITH INDUSTRY STANDARDS, AND OFFER ALL EMPLOYEES THE SAME BASIC BENEFITS (HEALTH INSURANCE, VACATION, PERSONAL TIME OFF, ETC.; APPROPRIATE ADDITIONAL BENEFITS FOR MANAGERS AND EXECUTIVES ARE ALWAYS AT COMPANY DISCRETION).

(The content that appears in the above table was adapted from the "Facilities Management Checklist" appearing in BOMI Institute's *Administration.*[5])

Note that many of the needs areas overlap to a certain extent when applying the Maslow model to management use, as seen in the table above. The goal for managers who use this model is to build on each employee's individual level of security (i.e., his or her met needs), thereby encouraging successive progression to the next level. For example, an employee who exhibits positive self-esteem should be ready to self-actualize.

---

[5]   "Facilities Management Checklist" adapted from BOMI Institute's *Administration,* www.bomiedu.org/12121.html; "Facilities Management Compliance Feature: Motivating Employees through Maslow's Hierarchy of Needs," http://www.fmlink.com/article.cgi?type=How%20To&title=Motivating%20Employees%2.

Now that we've explored how to best use the Maslow motivational model, let's turn our attention to the Herzberg model.

Frederick Herzberg's Model

Best known for his concept of "job enrichment" and his motivator-hygiene theory, Frederick Herzberg also had a powerful influence on twentieth-century management. Like Maslow, Herzberg believed that humans are motivated by both physiological and psychological needs. Herzberg's 1959 book, *The Motivation to Work*, describes a two-factor content theory (i.e., physiological and psychological needs), more commonly known as the *two-need system*.

Similar to the hierarchy of needs, the two-need system centers on human physiological/psychological needs and the ways in which they impact motivation. In Herzberg's model, the "hygiene" factors lead to (potential) dissatisfaction, while the "motivators" lead to (potential) satisfaction. His views on job enrichment recognized that every employee use his or her abilities to the utmost in order to feel fulfilled; in addition, employees who demonstrate ability should receive increased responsibility that reflects that ability, and should also be sufficiently challenged so that they continue to grow.

We can better understand the motivator-hygiene theory by studying the table below:

Hygiene Factors
Create dissatisfaction and demotivation when not present
• company policy
• supervision
• relationship with manager and higher-ups
• work conditions
• compensation (salary, benefits, etc.)
• relationships with peers (coworkers, team members, etc.)

Motivators
Create satisfaction and motivation when present
• achievement
• recognition
• enjoyment of the work itself
• responsibility
• advancement
• growth

(**NOTE:** *Table and explanatory text adapted from standard descriptions of Herzberg's motivational theory.*)

Hygiene and motivation factors are different but not opposing. We can think of the hygiene factors as maintaining certain basics that are required to keep employees from becoming dissatisfied. The motivating factors are much more fluid, which is why they continue to work effectively.

As with Maslow, a detailed discussion of Herzberg's theories would be beyond the scope and intention of this book. What we, as managers, need to concern ourselves with is how to use our knowledge of what fosters employee satisfaction and dissatisfaction in order to create an environment with more of the former and less of the latter.

Effective managers know that determining what motivates employees is the only way to positively impact their behavior.

Practical Application of the Herzberg Model

Below are some ideas for how management can use the Herzberg model to create a motivating workplace environment. (Of course we must always keep in mind that the management objective is not to directly motivate but to cause employees to self-motivate. Fear, incentives, and other short-term practices are rarely sustainable, as seen in the true-to-life business scenario at the beginning of this chapter.)

First, managers would be wise to remain aware of Herzberg's two-need system (physiological and psychological needs), as follows:

1. **physiological needs**—avoiding unpleasantness or discomfort (these needs may be fulfilled by salary [e.g., money to buy food, provide shelter, etc.])
2. **psychological needs**—achieving personal growth/development (these needs may be fulfilled by work activities [e.g., meeting the challenges that cause us to grow])

In addition, effective managers integrate the methods and techniques listed below:

- establishing open lines of communication with employees
- taking the time to listen to employees' ideas (remember that they have the deepest expert knowledge on the task at hand)
- learning to quickly identify talent in order to fast-track the promotions of high-potential employees
- cultivating a better understanding of individual employees' personal circumstances (developing and exhibiting empathy)

(The content that appears in the two lists above was adapted from the "Frederick Herzberg—Theory of Motivation," on *Training & Development Solutions [TDS].*[6])

Now that we've explored how to best utilize the Herzberg motivational model, let's turn our attention to Daniel Pink's model, which is very useful for managers in the twenty-first century.

Daniel Pink's *Drive* Model

In his groundbreaking 2009 book, *Drive: The Surprising Truth about What Motivates Us,* Daniel Pink presents the idea that "use of rewards and punishments to control our employees' production is an antiquated way

---

[6] "Frederick Herzberg—Theory of Motivation" *Training & Development Solutions (TDS),* http://www.trainanddevelop.co.uk/article/frederick-herzberg-theory-of-motivation-a78.

of managing people. To maximize their enjoyment and productivity for twenty-first century work, we need to upgrade our thinking to include autonomy, mastery, and purpose."[7]

Clearly, this model ties in with our discussion. *Autonomy* refers to empowering employees to make their own decisions; *mastery* refers to their increased performance; *purpose* refers to their actualized development. Of course all motivational models are just that: paradigms for managers to integrate into their techniques and methods—always with the primary aim of increasing employee performance, which is an indicator of managerial ability, and which also improves the company's bottom line.

As with Maslow and Herzberg, a detailed discussion of Pink's theories would be beyond the scope and intention of this book. What we, as managers, need to concern ourselves with is how to use the innovative theories in Pink's Drive model to upgrade our own techniques and methods for twenty-first-century effectiveness and success.

In essence, autonomy, mastery, and purpose simply reflect the ideal of the "right person in the right job." When we are empowered (autonomy), we are more likely to fulfill our highest potential and do our best (mastery), and, simultaneously, to act with honor and integrity (purpose).

Practical Application of Daniel Pink's Drive Model

Below are some ideas for how management can use the Drive model to create a motivating workplace environment. (Remember that the manager's objective is not to directly motivate employees, but to create an environment where employees feel valued and so will motivate themselves. This has never been more true than in the twenty-first century, with the technological advances, globalization, and virtual organizations that dominate the landscape—and that have changed the face of business forever.)

---

[7]   Daniel H. Pink, *Drive: The Surprising Truth about What Motivates Us* (New York: Riverhead, 2009).

Pink's Drive model rejects what he calls "carrots and sticks" (the twentieth-century punishment-and-reward systems still quite popular today) because these systems often lead to such unwanted results as

- destroying internal employee motivation (self-motivation);
- decreasing performance;
- destroying creativity and innovation;
- crowding out good behavior;
- encouraging cheating, shortcuts, and unethical behavior; and
- fostering short-term thinking.

(The content that appears in the above list was adapted from "What Really Motivates Us?" on the website Barking Up the Wrong Tree.[8])

By encouraging autonomy, mastery, and purpose, managers can avoid the negative outcomes reflected in the above list. To clarify, autonomy is not the same as independence. It is part of effective teamwork, because it requires the individual to freely choose and embrace empowerment. Autonomy also does not preclude accountability. Employees must always be accountable (and so must managers).

Simply stated, Pink's Drive model provides the most-effective "update" to the older motivational models because autonomy, mastery, and purpose are what we need in order to thrive in the twenty-first-century business world of globalization and virtual teamwork.

Our examination of the three motivational models discussed (Maslow, Herzberg, and Pink) makes it clear that motivation is a key management tool. In addition, each model underscores the effectiveness of the core statement opening this chapter: in order to positively influence or change employee behavior, managers must first determine what motivates employees. Finally, our discussion illustrates the ways in which motivation is linked to communication, strategic planning and goal setting, organizational structure, and employee development/advancement. To reemphasize,

---

[8]   "What Really Motivates Us?" Barking Up the Wrong Tree, http://www
       .bakadesuyo.com/2011/05/what-really-motivates-us/.

all the essential tools we've discussed throughout this book work most effectively when used in concert.

Effective management is simple, but it depends on the synergistic use of all the essential tools and techniques.

Applying What You Have Learned

As the core statement opening this chapter emphasizes, managers who want to positively influence or change employee behavior must start by determining what motivates employees. Any of the motivational models discussed (or a combination of two or all three) can help managers create an environment that fosters motivation, but the most important point to remember is that the manager's job is not to directly motivate, but to cause employees to motivate themselves. (Remember, short-term methods, such as fear or incentives, rarely have sustainable results.) In this century of hypertechnology, globalization, and virtual teams, encouraging employee self-motivation is a key management responsibility more so than ever before.

Here are some essential steps related to motivation that we all need to implement:

1. Utilize the key management tool of motivation to create an organizational climate that makes employees feel valued, empowered, and fulfilled. (Study and integrate the elements of the Maslow, Herzberg, and Pink models that will work best in your specific organization.)
2. Empower employees and encourage their self-motivation, as this will increase their performance, highlight your value as a manager, and improve the company's bottom line.
3. Establish effective motivational models, communicate them clearly, and cascade them appropriately throughout the organization.

By incorporating the above items 1 through 3 into our daily routine, we are well on the way to becoming effective managers. And that's "simply management"!

Now that we've thoroughly explored motivation, as well as the other essential tools and techniques that comprise the management tool kit, let's review and reinforce the most-important aspects of our discussion, which we will do in the conclusion that follows.

CONCLUSION

Throughout this book, we have explored the essential management tools and techniques that lead to enduring effectiveness as a manager in today's business world. We have discussed important management principles, but, as promised, we have honored the primary intention of this book: sharing my insights and experience as a CEO. Our observations of true-to-life business scenarios, followed by our analyses of the most-effective responses to the challenges portrayed therein, have helped us see the common pitfalls of day-to-day managing—as well as the best ways to avoid and transcend them. In short, we have examined the things effective managers should and should not do.

We have learned that, above all, managers must always remember that they are managers! Managers contribute to increased productivity and profitability by focusing on their managerial tasks and delegating other responsibilities and tasks to the appropriate support staff. Conversely, managers who impede productivity cannot increase profitability. And we all know that in business, nothing trumps the bottom line.

In recognition of the all of the foregoing, let's now review, reiterate, and reinforce what we have learned. The highlights of our discussion appear in the pages that follow.

The Management Tool Kit

1. Management Principles (Essence of Management)
2. Strategic Planning and Goal Setting
3. Organizational Structure

4. Governance and Controls
5. Employee Development and Advancement
6. Communication
7. Motivation

As described in the introduction, managerial success in the twenty-first century requires effective use of all the components in the management tool kit, as these tools and techniques are synergistic and work best when used in concert. Using the management tool kit with optimal effectiveness can help eliminate any current challenge, enabling ineffective managers to become good managers—and effective managers to become *great* managers.

Core Statements: Management Wisdom for Every Day

Incorporating the wisdom of each of the core statements below into our daily routine improves our effectiveness as managers:

Essence of Management	Managers provide an essential contribution to productivity as they focus on managerial tasks and delegate expert responsibilities.
Strategic Planning and Goal Setting	Strategic planning and goal setting should always be a group process.
Organizational Structure	Like all management tools, the organization tool is easy to use but often misunderstood.
Governance and Controls	Controls refer to the past; governance refers to the future.
Employee Development and Advancement	A manager's skill is best measured by increased employee performance.
Communication	Effective communication is strategic: it determines exactly who is to receive what information, when, how, and with what intention.
Motivation	If the manager wants to positively influence or change the behavior of his employee, there is only one starting point: determining what motivates the employee.

Daily Management Essentials

Integrating what we have learned into our daily routine is essential to ensuring our sustainable effectiveness and success as managers. The table below features some of the most-significant practical applications gleaned from our discussions:

Essence of Management	
Management Control Loop	Utilize the management control loop (the mechanism for using all the elements of the management tool kit).
Management versus Expert Tasks	Establish a balance between management tasks and expert (specialist) tasks.
Management Style	Recognize management style and adapt it as needed.
Strategic Planning and Goal Setting	
Group Process for Plans and Goals	Establish a group process for planning and goal setting in order to ensure employee buy-in.
Goal Alignment	Ensure goal alignment through appropriate cascade at all levels.
Change Management	Recognize the need for change and implement such changes effectively, ensuring short- and long-term success.
Organizational Structure	
Clear Management Triangles	Utilize the key management tool of organization, including effective management triangles and a clear system of decentralization or centralization (depending on company needs).
Unambiguous Chain of Command	Ensure clear line of authority and decision making, appropriately cascaded to all levels.
Effective Systems and Procedures	Establish effective systems and procedures for whichever type of organization the company uses (e.g., matrix, profit center, etc.), as well as the virtual teams that dominate the twenty-first-century business landscape.

Governance and Controls	
Employee Self-Monitoring	Utilize the key management tool of governance and controls, including future-oriented focus and employee empowerment and self-monitoring.
Clear Authority/ Decision Making	Ensure clear and unambiguous decision-making authority, appropriately cascaded to all levels.
Effective Governance System	Establish an effective governance system (framework and process), which will automatically lead to a minimal amount of time and effort spent on controls.
Employee Development and Advancement	
Effective Development Methods and Measurements	Utilize the key management tool of employee development and advancement, including effective methods and measurements (continual dialoguing with employees, plus a formal evaluation system).
Employee Empowerment	Empower employees to make decisions and provide the necessary support to allow them to do so with confidence and effectiveness.
Development, Advancement, and Mentorship	Establish the clear differences between development and advancement, and between advancement and promotion, and encourage employees to seek and obtain mentorship, as appropriate.
Communication	
Clear and Concise Communication	Utilize the key management tool of communication to ensure that all information and messages are concise, purposeful, and unambiguous. (Strategic communication plans, e-mail guidelines, global communication guidelines, and other best-practice methods assist in ensuring that information flows smoothly and efficiently.)
Effective Employee Communicators	Empower employees to be effective communicators, and provide the necessary support to allow them to do so (using the methods described, as well as any others that prove beneficial, useful, and effective).

Unambiguous Communication Guidelines	Establish communication guidelines and expectations, and cascade them appropriately to all levels within each management triangle and the organization as a whole.
Motivation	
Create a Motivating Environment	Utilize the key management tool of motivation to create an organizational climate that makes employees feel valued, empowered, and fulfilled.
Encourage Employee Self-Motivation	Empower employees and encourage their self-motivation, as this will increase their performance, highlight your value as a manager, and improve the company's bottom line.
Effective Motivational Models	Establish effective motivational models, communicate them clearly, and cascade them appropriately throughout the organization.

The items listed in the table above reflect the management tool kit. Remember that these are essential management tools and techniques that all managers must use to optimal effect and never delegate. Following these principles and integrating them into our day-to-day managerial behavior is essential to success in the atmosphere of globalization, advanced technology, and virtual teams that dominate the twenty-first-century business landscape.

At the end of the introduction, I invited you to join me on the journey to becoming a more-effective manager. We have reached the end of this book, but the journey has only just begun. By incorporating all that we have discussed into our routine practice, we are well on the way to effective daily leadership, and that is a perpetually rewarding pursuit indeed. It's also "simply management"!

(**NOTE:** *For ease of use, and to help make this book a perennial go-to resource, the seven core statements highlighted earlier in this section appear at the beginning of their respective chapters, just below the chapter number and chapter title. A summary of the advice and suggestions given appears at the end of each chapter, in the "Applying What You Have Learned" sections. You can turn to any of these individual chapters, or to this conclusion, any time you need a refresher or reinforcement.*)

REFERENCES

"Communication: Various Best-Practices Research." http://onlinemba.unc .edu/research-and-insights/developing-real-skills-for-virtual-teams/ virtual-team-challenges/.

"Facilities Management Checklist," adapted from BOMI Institute's *Administration,* www.bomiedu.org/12121.html.

"Facilities Management Compliance Feature: Motivating Employees through Maslow's Hierarchy of Needs." http://www.fmlink.com/article .cgi?type=How%20To&title=Motivating%20Employees%2.

"Fifteen Tips for Writing Effective E-mail." *Think Simple Now.* http:// thinksimplenow.com/productivity/15-tips-for-writing-effective-email/.

"Frederick Herzberg—Theory of Motivation." *Training & Development Solutions (TDS).* http://www.trainanddevelop.co.uk/article/frederick-herzberg-theory-of-motivation-a78.

Herzberg, Frederick I. *The Motivation to Work.* New York: John Wiley and Sons, 1959.

Inscape Publishing. *Everything DiSC.* Minneapolis: Inscape Publishing, 2007–12.

Keirsey, David. *Please Understand Me II.* Del Mar, CA: Prometheus Nemesis Book Company, 1998.

Maslow, Abraham H. *Motivation and Personality.* New York: Harper, 1954.

McCrae, R. R., and P. T. Costa. "Reinterpreting the Myers-Briggs Type Indicator from the Perspective of the Five-Factor Model of Personality," *Journal of Personality* 57, no. 1 (1989): 17–40. doi:10.1111/j.1467-6494.1989.tb00759.x.

Myers, Isabel Briggs, with Peter B. Myers. *Gifts Differing: Understanding Personality Type.* Mountain View, CA: CCP, 1995.

Pink, Daniel H. *Drive: The Surprising Truth about What Motivates Us.* New York: Riverhead, 2009.

"What Really Motivates Us?" *Barking Up the Wrong Tree.* http://www.bakadesuyo.com/2011/05/what-really-motivates-us/.

ABOUT THE AUTHOR

Martin H. Richenhagen has been president and chief executive officer (CEO) of AGCO Corporation since March 2004, following his selection by the board of directors. In August 2006 he was also appointed chairman of the board and continues to serve on the executive committee and the succession planning committee.

Prior to his tenure at AGCO, Mr. Richenhagen was the executive vice president of Forbo International SA, a manufacturing firm headquartered in Switzerland. He also served as group president for CLAAS KgaA mbH, a global manufacturer of agricultural equipment headquartered in Germany. Before that, Mr. Richenhagen was the senior executive vice president of field operations for Schindler Holding GmbH in Germany.

From 2006 through the first quarter of 2007 (when it was sold to Freeport-McMoRan Copper & Gold Inc.), Mr. Richenhagen served as a board member for the Phelps Dodge Corporation on the audit, finance, and corporate governance committees. He is currently a board member for PPG Industries, a leading coatings and specialty products and services company, where he also sits on the audit and technology & environment committees. Mr. Richenhagen is a member of the board of directors of the US Chamber of Commerce. He has served as chairman of the board of the Association of Equipment Manufacturers (AEM) and is a Life Honorary Director of AEM.

Over the course of two decades, his manufacturing career has covered a wide array of executive positions and managing directorships with responsibility for sales, marketing, human resources management, acquisitions, joint ventures, logistics, materials purchase, inventory management, and competitor intelligence.

An international business executive, Mr. Richenhagen is fluent in several languages and has spent many years living overseas. He is a graduate of the University of Bonn. In December 2008, Mr. Richenhagen was appointed honorary professor to the faculty of agricultural machinery at the TU Dresden, Dresden University of Technology (Germany).

As described in the preface, he wrote this book to share his knowledge, experience, and wisdom as a CEO with managers of all levels.

ABOUT AGCO

AGCO was established in 1990, with the purchase of Deutz Allis Corporation from Germany-based Kloeckner-Humboldt-Deutz AG. With roots firmly established in the farm equipment industry, AGCO's brand heritage reaches back to the mid-1800s. AGCO's current brands include Challenger, Fendt, GSI, Massey Fergusson, and Valtra.

Since its founding, AGCO has become a worldwide farm machinery company through market growth, strategic acquisitions, and cutting-edge agricultural solutions. AGCO has invested in North American manufacturing by expanding high horsepower wheeled tractor manufacturing production in Jackson, Minnesota (also the site of the company's state-of-the-art visitor center).

Listed on the New York Stock Exchange (NYSE) under the symbol "AGCO," AGCO continues to thrive as an industry leader and a Fortune 500 company.

To learn more about AGCO, please visit www.agcocorp.com.

INDEX

A

accuracy, as key segment of workplace behaviors, 9, 13

action as key segment of workplace behaviors, 10, 13

advanced technology, 106, 125

advancement, 9, 68–69, 74, 75, 77, 82–87, 115, 122, 124. *See also* promotions

assumptions, 22

authoritarian management style, 11

autonomy, in Daniel Pink's Drive model, 117

B

back delegate, 86

belongingness needs, in Maslow's hierarchy of needs, 112

budgets, 23–24

buffer zones, 7

burnout, 7

business segment organization, 49

buy-in, 17, 28, 30, 59, 74, 123

C

carrots and sticks, 118

central service departments, 45

central training departments, 84

centralization, 37–40, 123

chain of command, 3, 33, 43, 54, 57, 123

challenges, as key segment of workplace behaviors, 11, 13

change management, 29–31, 51, 123

collaboration, as key segment of workplace behaviors, 11, 13

collaborative planning, 27–28

communication

    choosing right method of, 98–99

    core statement about, 89, 122

    daily management essentials, 124–25

    definition, 89–90

    between global teams, 96–97

    goals, 99

    impact of little to no, 8

    as management tool, xviii, 4, 102–3

    pitfalls among receivers, 101

    pitfalls among senders, 101

    plans, 102

    principles of, 100–101

    technology and, 94–95, 99

    true-to-life business scenarios, 90–93

    in the twenty-first century, 93–94

    between virtual teams, 97–98

company as family, 46

computerization, 42, 52
conference calls, 94, 99
consensual decision-making method, 28
control loop, 3, 14, 123
controls
 assessment of, 63
 core statement about, 54, 122
 daily management essentials, 124
 definition, 54, 57, 62
 as management tool, xviii, 4
 percent of time spent on, 57, 59
 principles of, 64
 process, 65–66
 requirements of effective system of, 66
 true-to-life business scenarios, 55–56
cooperative management style, 11
core statements
 communication, 89, 122
 employee development and advancement, 68, 122
 essence of management, 1, 122
 governance and controls, 54, 122
 motivation, 105, 122
 organizational structure, 33, 122
 strategic planning and goal setting, 15, 122
corporate ideals, 20

D

daily management essentials, 123–25
day-to-day operations, 28, 40
decentralization, 37–40, 44, 50, 53, 123
decision-making authority, 3, 23, 38, 43, 45, 47, 48, 50, 54, 57–60, 64–67, 83, 84, 87, 124
decision-making process, 18

delegating, xvii, 1, 5–7, 9, 29, 38, 40, 43, 60, 62, 73, 83, 84, 121, 122, 125
departments, 42, 46
divisional organizations, 41
dreams, compared to goals, 18
Drive model, 116–18
Drive: The Surprising Truth about What Motivates Us (Pink), 116

E

earned recognition, 9
e-mails, 93–96, 98, 99, 124
employee advancement. *See also* advancement
 basics of, 82–83
 core statement about, 68, 122
 daily management essentials, 124
 definition, 68
 as management tool, xviii, 4
 tips for more productive talks about, 85–87
employee buy-in, 17, 28, 30, 59, 74, 123
employee development
 core statement about, 68, 122
 daily management essentials, 124
 definition, 68
 as management tool, xviii, 4
 measurements, 74–76, 124
 methods, 71–73, 124
 obstacles to, 83–85
 tips for more productive talks about, 85–87
 true-to-life business scenarios, 69–71
employee empowerment, 58, 59, 65, 83–84, 117, 124
employee evaluations, 76–82, 86
employee self-monitoring, 124

employee self-motivation, 105, 110, 111, 119, 125

empowerment, 58, 59, 65, 83–84, 117, 124

enthusiasm, as key segment of workplace behaviors, 11, 13

environment, 52

essence of management
core statement about, 1, 122
daily management essentials, 123
as management tool, xviii, 1–14

evaluation process, 78, 82, 84. *See also* employee evaluations; informal evaluation; spontaneous evaluations

Everything DiSC, 9–10, 13

excessive work hours, short-term, 8

expert tasks, versus management tasks, 4–9, 14, 123

external environment, assessment of, 21

F

face-to-face conversations, 95, 98

flattened hierarchy, 48

flexibility, 50–52, 93

functional organizational structure, 43–45, 48

functions
definition, 42–43
vertical administrative functions, 48

G

global teams, 96–97

globalization, 15, 27, 38, 44, 65, 75, 85, 106, 117–19, 125

goal alignment, 27, 123

goal setting
as continuous process, 18
core statement about, 15, 122

daily management essentials, 123

definition, 15

as group process, 15, 19, 22, 26, 27, 31, 123

as management tool, xviii

obstacles to, 26–27

process model, 19–25

as referring to future impact of today's decisions, 19

true-to-life business scenarios, 16–17

goals
and assumptions, 22
compared to objectives, 21
definition, 15, 18, 22, 25
SMART goals, 26

governance
core statement about, 54, 122
daily management essentials, 124
definition, 54, 56–57
framework, 57–58
as management tool, xviii, 4
percent of time spent on, 57, 59
principles of, 59–60
process, 58
requirements of effective system of, 63–64
results of, 62–63
system of, 124
true-to-life business scenarios, 55–56

guidelines, 23, 39, 49, 51, 99, 100, 124, 125

H

Herzberg, Frederick, 109

Herzberg's model, 114–16

horizontal tasks, areas, processes, and/ or projects, 48

hygiene factors, 114, 115
hyperconnectivity, 43
hypertechnology, 45, 119

I

"ideal" employee, 73
ideal performance evaluation system, 76–77
informal evaluation, 85
information overload, 101
innovation, 26, 52
instant messaging, 93, 98
integrated style of management, 13
Internet, 25, 31, 43, 52

J

job enrichment, 114

K

Keirsey Personality Sorter, 9

L

landscape analysis, 21

M

management, definition, 1
management behavior, styles of, 13–14
management by exception, 60–62
management control loop, 3, 123
management styles, 9–11, 123
management tasks, versus expert tasks, 4–9, 14, 123
management tool kit, xvii–xviii, 121–22
management tools, selection of, 4
management training and development, 5, 7, 8, 57
management triangle, 23, 24, 37, 40, 45, 52, 102–3, 123, 125

management wisdom, 122
mandatory evaluation systems, 76
Maslow, Abraham, 109
Maslow model, 110–13
Maslow's hierarchy of needs, 110
mastery, in Daniel Pink's Drive model, 117, 118
matrix organizational structure, 34–36
matrix organizations, 17, 41, 48–49
MBTI (Myers-Briggs Type Indicator), 9
McCrae/Costa "Big Five," 9
mentorship, 71, 72, 73, 85, 124
micromanaging, 65
mission, 20, 23, 31
mistakes, 57, 65–66, 72, 83, 86, 87
motivation
  core statement about, 105, 122
  daily management essentials, 125
  definition, 105–6
  as management tool, xviii, 4, 109
  models, 109
  teams as centered on, 46
  true-to-life business scenarios, 106–8
The Motivation to Work (Herzberg), 114
motivator-hygiene theory, 114–15
Myers-Briggs Type Indicator (MBTI), 9

N

natural ability, 9

O

objectives, 21
one-on-one communication, 94, 99
onsite employment, 52
organizational structure

changes in, 41
core statement about, 33, 122
daily management essentials, 123
definition, 33, 40
described, 3
effective systems/procedures, 123
guidelines for evaluating
  effectiveness of, 51
as management tool, xviii
true-to-life business scenarios,
  34–36
organizational units, 41
organizations
  divisional organizations, 41
  matrix organizations, 17, 41, 48–49
  project organizations, 47–48
  staff/line organizations, 41, 44–46
  team organizations, 41
  types of, 37
  virtual organizations, 117

P

performance, 68, 73, 85, 87
performance assessments, 63, 66
performance evaluations, 76–82
personal satisfaction, 71
personality traits, 10
personality-type paradigms/sorters,
  9–10
physiological needs
  in Herzberg's model, 116
  in Maslow's hierarchy of needs, 113
Pink, Daniel, 109, 116–17
Pink's Drive model, 116–18
planning
  collaborative planning, 27–28
  responsibilities, 29
  strategic planning. *See* strategic
    planning

techniques, 24–25
policies-and-procedures manual, 23
pricing tables, 23
product portfolio, 22
productivity, xvii, 1, 4, 5, 46, 50, 52, 71,
  95, 117, 121, 122
professional skill, 9
profit centers, 41, 49–52, 123
profit potential, 21
profitability, xvii, 4, 51, 121
project organizations, 47–48
promotions, 5–7, 9, 68, 82, 83, 124
psychological needs, in Maslow's
  hierarchy of needs, 116
punishment-and-reward system, 118
purpose, in Daniel Pink's Drive model,
  117, 118

R

recognition, earned, 9
regional segmentation, 41
relationship orientation (RO), 12–13
relationship style of management, 13
result centers, 50
results
  governance results, 62–63
  as key segment of workplace
    behaviors, 10, 13
  responsibility for, 3
rewards, 6, 7, 9, 116, 118, 125
right person in the right job, 73, 117
RO (relationship orientation), 12–13

S

salary-increase discussions, 87
security needs, in Maslow's hierarchy
  of needs, 113
segmentation based on function, 41
self-actualization needs, in Maslow's

hierarchy of needs, 111
self-esteem needs, in Maslow's
hierarchy of needs, 112
self-monitoring, 124
self-motivation, 105, 110, 111, 119, 125
situational management, 10–13
SMART goals, 26
smartphones, 31, 94, 95
social media, 31, 52
spontaneous evaluations, 85
stability, as key segment of workplace
behaviors, 10, 13
staff, 44
staff departments, 44–45
staff/line organizations, 41, 44–46
strategic planning
as continuous process, 18
core statement about, 15, 122
daily management essentials, 123
definition, 15
as group process, 25, 27–28, 30, 31,
123
as management tool, xviii, 3
obstacles to, 26–27
process model, 19–25
as referring to future impact of
today's decisions, 19
tools, 18
true-to-life business scenarios,
16–17
strengths, analysis of, 21
structuring elements, 41
support, as key segment of workplace
behaviors, 10, 13

T
task orientation (TO), 12–13
task style of management, 13
team organizations, 41

team satisfaction, 72
teams, 46–47
teamwork, 11, 26–28, 96, 107, 118
technology
advanced technology, 106, 125
and effective communication,
94–95, 99
hypertechnology, 45, 119
telecommuting, 11, 15, 27, 43, 46, 52,
96, 98
texting, 93, 94, 95, 98, 99
TO (task orientation), 12–13
tolerance levels, 60
training
central training departments, 84
management training and
development, 5, 7, 8, 57
triangle principle, 37. *See also*
management triangle
true-to-life business scenarios
effective governance and controls
are key to company success, 55–56
effective method of employee
development, 69–70
effective methods of motivating
employees, 106–8
effective methods of strategic
communication, 90–93
focusing on managerial tasks by
delegating expert responsibilities,
2
global matrix organizational
structure, 34–36
ineffective method of employee
development, 70–71
strategic planning and goal setting
as a group process, 16–17
two-need system, 114, 116

V

vertical administrative functions, 48
video conferences, 94, 95, 97, 98, 99
virtual organizations, 117
virtual teams, 38, 43, 44, 46, 51–52, 56,
  65, 75, 85, 96, 97–98, 103, 106, 118,
  123, 125
vision, 20, 23, 31

W

weaknesses, analysis of, 21
work overload, 7
workplace behaviors, key segments of,
  9–10, 13